DATE DUE

TRANS-ATLANTIC HISTORICAL
SOLIDARITY

TRANS-ATLANTIC HISTORICAL SOLIDARITY

LECTURES DELIVERED BEFORE THE
UNIVERSITY OF OXFORD IN EASTER
AND TRINITY TERMS 1913

BY

CHARLES FRANCIS ADAMS

OXFORD
AT THE CLARENDON PRESS
1913

OXFORD UNIVERSITY PRESS
LONDON EDINBURGH GLASGOW NEW YORK
TORONTO MELBOURNE BOMBAY
HUMPHREY MILFORD
PUBLISHER TO THE UNIVERSITY

CONTENTS

		PAGE
	INTRODUCTORY	9
I.	PRINCIPIA	25
II.	THE CONFEDERATE COTTON CAMPAIGN, LANCASHIRE, 1861–62	55
III.	DIS ALITER VISUM	85
IV.	A GREAT HISTORICAL CHARACTER AND VAE VICTIS	131
	INDEX	181

'There is apparently much truth in the belief that the wonderful progress of the United States, as well as the character of the people, are the results of natural selection; for the more energetic, restless, and courageous men from all parts of Europe have emigrated during the last ten or twelve generations to that great country, and have there succeeded best. Looking to the distant future, I do not think that the Rev. Mr. Zincke takes an exaggerated view when he says: "All other series of events—as that which resulted in the culture of mind in Greece, and that which resulted in the empire of Rome—only appear to have purpose and value when viewed in connexion with, or rather as subsidiary to . . . the great stream of Anglo-Saxon emigration to the west."'—DARWIN, *The Descent of Man*, Chapter V.

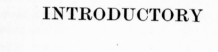

INTRODUCTORY

INTRODUCTORY [1]

THE Annual Lectures, of which the following is the Second Course, were only recently provided for, largely through the influence of Oxford professors and instructors who, in pursuance of their calling, had on invitation visited America. They are an outcome of the great Rhodes Scholarship Foundation. Last year Mr. James Ford Rhodes, the well-known American historian, bearing the same patronymic but in no way connected with the South African notability, was selected—and most properly selected —to initiate the Lectureship. This he did, delivering three lectures, since published in book form.[2] When invited to deliver the course in succession to Mr. Rhodes, I was informed that the number of lectures was a matter resting with me, with a single limitation: I was not to discourse on history in the abstract, or on historical themes in general, but confine myself to American history or American historical topics;—a restriction which wholly commended itself to my own judgement. After giving the matter as careful consideration as was then in my power, I decided on a course of four lectures. I did not see how in any less space I could deal properly

[1] From the *Proceedings* of the *Massachusetts Historical Society* for June, 1913. Vol. 46, pp. 432–40.
[2] *Lectures on the American Civil War.* The Macmillan Company, 1913.

with the topics which suggested themselves; in fact, as the result showed, six or seven or even eight lectures would have scarcely sufficed for their proper treatment.

Naturally, during the winter of 1912–13, between the acceptance of the invitation and my sailing for England, the subject was more or less constantly in my mind. Passing the season in Washington, it was, also, my fortune to see a good deal of Mr. James Bryce, then British Ambassador. Mr. Bryce, moreover, evinced a very considerable interest in my proposed course, having for many years been himself an Oxford lecturer. One day, when taking a long stroll together through the streets of Washington, he took occasion to inquire as to the topics with which I proposed to deal, and my method of treatment. I at once told him that my main thesis would be certain phases of what we in America term 'The Civil War'—that is, the struggle which, convulsing the United States, attracted the attention of the whole civilized world during the four years between April, 1861, and April, 1865. I was surprised, and somewhat taken aback by what followed. In the gentlest possible way—most diplomatically, I might say— Mr. Bryce proceeded to intimate that I would probably find an English audience of the present generation, especially an Oxford lecture audience, quite uninformed on everything connected with our Civil War; which, indeed, had now become to the people of Great Britain somewhat remotely historical. In other words, it was implied that our great

American conflict of half a century back, which looms so large in American memory, had quite passed out of English recollection, and there takes its place with other episodes of a character more or less important which have since occupied, and, at the moment, perhaps engrossed public attention. Occurring at different times and in many countries, these, Mr. Bryce intimated, had now followed each other into oblivion; and our great ordeal had proved no exception to the general rule.

> Time hath, my lord, a wallet on his back,
> Wherein he puts alms for oblivion;

and, so far as an Oxford audience was concerned, to Time's wallet I found my topic by high authority comfortably assigned.

While, however, conveying to me in guarded terms this not altogether palatable intimation, Mr. Bryce added the qualifying remark that at the time—that is, during the period between 1861 and 1865, he then being a recent Oxford graduate—the incidents of the struggle as it progressed had excited deeper interest in England, especially in social and political circles in London and Oxford, than any event of a similar character which has since occurred. He even went so far as to say that so intense was the interest felt over that struggle, the numerous partisans of the South arraying themselves against the few who sympathized with the North, that discussions were discouraged. At the dinner table, for instance, passages occurred marked by acrimony and even rudeness. The ordinary social amenities were altogether too frequently

disregarded.[1] This he distinctly recalled; and what
he said confirmed my own personal, and in some
connexions my own irritating, recollection.

There was, however, another observation of Mr.
Bryce, made by him on the same or some similar
occasion, to which also I must now refer. He intimated, again in diplomatic fashion, a decided doubt
whether the conflict in question would, as an historical
episode and incident in the great evolutionary record,
hereafter loom up in the same large proportions it always
must bear in the minds of those of the American generation directly concerned in it—the generation to
which I personally belong. The issues, he more than
hinted, were in his judgement either of no great fundamental importance, or, in the case of slavery, already
foregone conclusions; and the personages who figured
in the struggle would, he thought, become less and less
considered with the lapse of time. Finally, he more
than implied a personal belief that the memorials we
had created to them would not infrequently call for
explanation.

This was to me a novel point of view; and then,
and subsequently while preparing my lectures in
London, I gave no inconsiderable thought to it. After
all, might it not be as Mr. Bryce said? Nations, like
individuals, are always prone to magnify themselves
and the importance of events in which they have been
concerned. Above all, going to Oxford to deliver
a course of lectures, to a degree international in
character, it behoved me to avoid anything which

[1] See Note 1, p. 18.

might seem grandiose—the eagle must emit no semblance even of a scream! On this score, therefore, Mr. Bryce's intimations gave rise in me to no little perplexity, and, subsequently, imposed a very considerable amount of labour, revisionary in character. In fact, I threw aside nearly all the material prepared in America, and, starting afresh, groped my way, so to speak, as I went on, all the while studying a British environment. As finally delivered, therefore, my lectures were in purport altogether different from those I had proposed to deliver. Still, in the close I wholly failed in one respect to concur in Mr. Bryce's judgement; for the more I reflected on the matter from the point of view he had suggested, the more I felt convinced that, as the years rolled by and the generations passed on, the conflict he had referred to as now forgotten in Europe would assume ever larger world-proportions and become matter of more careful general study. In a word, our American Civil War would, when the final verdict is rendered, loom large, and become an accepted episode of first-class and world-wide moment. Its broad dramatic features will also be recognized.

This spirit more and more possessing me, I prepared the following lectures in the course of their delivery. So far as the issues involved in our struggle, and in some cases therein decided, were concerned, I felt I was teaching school. Of those issues I found myself impelled to emphasize at least three. First was the process and consummation of a national crystallization. The formal entry on the world-stage of

a power admittedly of the first class—whether
Prussia, Italy, Germany or the United States—is not,
I submit, an incident of secondary historical importance. It is not likely to be ignored by the historian,
much less forgotten. Such, however, was the direct
outcome of our American War. The next issue of
importance decided in that conflict—Chattel Humanity—was also a world-issue, which goes back to the
very beginning—literally, to the Book of Genesis;
for, to any one at all acquainted with even scriptural
narrative, the fact that human servitude has existed
from the commencement admits of no question. That
in 1860 slavery as an institution was becoming subject
to greater and greater recognized limitations is indisputable; as also that among the nations of the world
of more advanced civilization it had ceased to exist.
That it was then a doomed system we now see. So
far as the African was concerned, however, down to
1862 negro slavery was a recognized and accepted
institution, certain exceptional countries alone having
outlawed it. Lincoln's Proclamation of Emancipation,
one of the most dramatic acts in the history of mankind, thus literally struck from man the shackles of
chattelism, irrespective of race or hue. This I submit
was another by no means inconsiderable outcome, and
one not likely to be permanently forgotten.[2]

Nor was the next issue of less importance than
those already specified: I refer to the world-
movement towards what is now known as Democracy.
That issue was very directly involved in our struggle.

[2] See Note 2, p. 19.

This no more admits of denial than that Democracy is an issue now much in evidence in European as well as American political activities, and more especially in those of Great Britain. It may be described in fact as the political issue of to-day, tending toward Collectivism, as it is called, and through that to Socialism. That this tendency received a pronounced impetus as one of the outcomes of our war, I take to be so indisputable as to call merely for mention.[3] Posterity will probably have occasion to bear the fact freshly in mind.

Thus, Mr. Bryce to the contrary notwithstanding, as I meditated the matter in London no less than three issues of Trans-Atlantic Historical Solidarity of first-class historical significance suggested themselves for my Oxford course; first, United States nationality; second, the end of slavery, or property in man; third, the evolution, if it may be so called, of Democracy. These, moreover, were what may be described as civil issues only. But when it came to military and naval considerations, the importance of the struggle was no less marked. In fact, it there assumed largest immediate proportions and an emphasis most dramatically pronounced; for, whether by sea or by land, it revolutionized warfare. As respects maritime operations, this admitted of no sort of question. The British navy of the Crimean war passed out of existence, and was consigned, so to speak, to the junk heap, when the old-style United States 40-gun steam frigate *Merrimac*, crudely remodelled into a nonde-

[3] See Note 3, p. 21.

script iron-shedded Confederate floating battery and
steam-ram, now called the *Virginia*, made its way
from Norfolk to Fortress Monroe in early March,
1862, there unexpectedly encountering the newly
devised armoured and turreted United States steam-
battery *Monitor*. Before that affair the navies of the
world were made up of wooden sailing-ships with,
perhaps, auxiliary steam-power; out of it emerged
the super-Dreadnought. A revolution in naval archi-
tecture and tactics had in a single day been
worked no less radical than that brought about
by Drake and the British mariners through their
windward manœuvring in the conflict with the
Spanish Armada three hundred years before. It is
no exaggeration to say that the action in Hampton
Roads in March, 1862, bore the same relation to
the attack of the combined British-French fleets on
the defences of Sebastopol in October, 1854, that the
destruction of the Armada in 1588 bore to the battle
of Lepanto in 1571.

It was, moreover, the same in military operations.
During our war, as other nations have since learned,
the discovery and application of the breechloader and
magazine gun rendered frontal attacks, assuming
opponents in some degree equally matched, impossible
of success. The tactics of Napoleon were remitted to
the past of Alexander.

Thus, in spite of the doubts suggested by Mr.
Bryce, my more mature reflection satisfied me that it
was fairly a matter of question whether any conflict
ever waged between men on earth had been more

momentous, and fruitful of results both immediate and remote, than that in which, between 1861 and 1865, it had been given me to participate.

It was with this conviction I warmed to my work, feeling my way, so to speak, as I went along; for after reaching London it was forced upon me that I was addressing an audience quite uninformed on the subjects with which I was to deal, and little interested therein. Historically and otherwise the minds of those composing it were intent on events either of the more remote past or now elsewhere in progress. Their faces were turned to the East. In a word, so far as the prescribed subject of my course was concerned, my listeners had to be educated, starting with the elementary.

My effort, therefore, throughout was to develop the close, at times the dramatic, connexion of the events with which I dealt with the history proper of those I addressed, or with history at the moment making. I selected accordingly; with what degree of success remains to be passed upon by others. The ordeal, I freely confess, I had not anticipated; nor would I care to be called upon again to face one similar. In passing through it, moreover, I found myself compelled to omit, as impossible of condensation and use within the time allotted me, a large amount of material very necessary, from my point of view, to a correct understanding of the topics with which I dealt. The matter thus put aside was indeed fully equal in amount to that used. A portion of it is included in the present publication. My object has been to impress such as may study this, the second course in the Oxford American Lectureship, with a sense not only of the importance of our American history in connexion with that of Great Britain, of Europe, and of mankind, but of the far-reaching world-wide influence it both has already exerted and is manifestly destined hereafter to exert.

Note 1, Page 12.

'There was a time when, in the great American Civil War, the sympathies of the English upper classes went with slavery, and when the North had scant justice and no mercy at their hands. I have myself seen that most distinguished man, Charles Francis Adams, subjected in society to treatment which, if he had resented it, might have seriously imperilled the relations of the two countries; and which nothing but the wonderful self-command of a very strong man, and his resolute determination to stifle all personal feeling, and to consider himself only as the Minister of a great country, enabled him to treat, as he did, with mute disdain. But in this critical state of things in and out of Parliament, Mr. Disraeli and Sir Stafford Northcote on one side, and the Duke of Argyll and Sir George Cornewall Lewis on the other, mainly contributed to keep this country neutral, and to save us from the ruinous mistake of taking part with the South.' (Quoted in Andrew Lang's *Life, Letters, and Diaries of Sir Stafford Northcote, First Earl of Iddesleigh*, p. 113, from an article by Lord Chief Justice Coleridge in *Macmillan's Magazine*, January, 1888.)

'Assuming, however, that they did understand this, there is still a good deal to be explained about the state of English opinion which it is rather hard to put plainly to them. I really don't know how to translate into civil language what I have heard a thousand times over in England that both sides are such a set of snobs and blackguards that we only

wish they could both be licked; or that their armies are the
scum of the earth, and the war got up by contractors; or that
the race is altogether degenerate and demoralized, and it is
pleasant to see such a set of bullies have a fall. I really
can't tell them all these little compliments, which I have
heard in private conversation word for word, and which are
a free translation of *Times* and *Saturday Review*, even
if I introduce them with [the] apology (though it is a really
genuine apology) that we know nothing at all about them."
(From a letter to his mother, Lady Stephen, written by
Leslie Stephen from Washington, in September, 1863.
Quoted by Prof. Maitland in the *Life and Letters of Leslie
Stephen*, p. 122.)

NOTE 2, PAGE 14.

The issue of *Fraser's Magazine* for February, 1862,
contained (pp. 257–68) a paper by John Stuart Mill
entitled 'The Contest in America'. It is to be borne
in mind that Mr. Mill in preparing this paper wrote
eight months before President Lincoln made the
earliest announcement of his intention to issue a Proclamation of Emancipation, and at a time when a large
and influential party in Great Britain insisted upon it
that neither slavery nor the emancipation of the slave
in any way entered as a considerable factor into the
struggle then going on in America. With singular
foresight and sagacity, and a remarkable insight into
the American situation, Mr. Mill observed in this
paper:

'But the parties in a protracted civil war almost invariably
end by taking more extreme, not to say higher grounds of
principle, than they began with. Middle parties and friends
of compromise are soon left behind; and if the writers who so

severely criticize the present moderation of the Free-soilers are desirous to see the war become an abolition war, it is probable that if the war lasts long enough they will be gratified. Without the smallest pretension to see farther into futurity than other people, I at least have foreseen and fore-told from the first, that if the South were not promptly put down, the contest would become distinctly an anti-slavery one; nor do I believe that any person, accustomed to reflect on the course of human affairs in troubled times, can expect anything else. Those who have read, even cursorily, the most valuable testimony to which the English public have access, concerning the real state of affairs in America—the letters of the *Times* correspondent, Mr. Russell—must have observed how early and rapidly he arrived at the same con-clusion, and with what increasing emphasis he now continually reiterates it. In one of his recent letters he names the end of next summer as the period by which, if the war has not sooner terminated, it will have assumed a complete anti-slavery character. So early a term exceeds, I confess, my most sanguine hopes; but if Mr. Russell be right, heaven forbid that the war should cease sooner, for if it lasts till then it is quite possible that it will regenerate the American people. . . . As long as justice and injustice have not terminated *their* ever-renewing fight for ascendancy in the affairs of mankind, human beings must be willing, when need is, to do battle for the one against the other. I am far from saying that the present struggle, on the part of the Northern Americans, is wholly of this exalted character; that it has arrived at the stage of being altogether a war for justice, a war of principle. But there was from the beginning, and now is, a large infusion of that element in it; and this is increasing, will increase, and if the war lasts, will in the end predominate. Should that time come, not only will the greatest enormity which still exists among mankind as an institution receive far earlier its *coup de grâce* than there has ever, until now, appeared any probability of; but in effecting this the Free States will have raised themselves to that elevated position in the scale of morality and dignity, which is derived from great

sacrifices consciously made in a virtuous cause, and the sense
of an inestimable benefit to all future ages, brought about by
their own voluntary efforts.'

Note 3, Page 15.

In the early months of 1863, following the Proclamation of Emancipation and the disasters suffered
by the Army of the Potomac while under the command of General Burnside, who had replaced General
McClellan, there was a reactionary wave of Conservatism in Great Britain. This movement and
its connexion with events in America was editorially
referred to in *Blackwood's Edinburgh Magazine* for February, 1863, as follows :

It is a not less remarkable feature of the times that in
politics also all England now is nearly of one mind. . . . It is
a mistake to attribute this universal Conservatism to the
breakdown of democratic institutions in America. The
" Conservative reaction ", to adopt the common but exception-
able phrase, had unmistakably manifested itself before a single
shot had been fired in America—before the bloodless bombardment of Fort Sumter announced the approach of that
deplorable conflict which has served to expose Democracy in
its worst and most contemptible form, and to reveal, in the
bosom of republican America, a mass of corruption, imbeci-
lity, meanness, and malignity, which, taken together, have
never been equalled in the whole world. But if a Conservative feeling had been steadily growing up in England before
the " bursting of the American bubble ", it is equally true that
that great collapse of Democracy has done much to give
to that feeling its present universality. Abstract reasoning
cannot affect mankind with the same force as actual experi-
ment and practical demonstration. Every sensible man in
this country now acknowledges—what nearly all sensible

men for some years past felt, but lacked the courage to say—
that we have already gone as far towards Democracy as it is
safe to go, and that another step like that proposed by Lord
Russell would have carried us irretrievably over the precipice.
This is the great moral benefit which we have derived from
the events in America.

  . . . This is a free country, and a few eloquent or blustering
Radicals serve to " let off the steam " of their class, and serve
to remind the sober-minded portion of the community what
a very mad and drunken thing Radicalism is.   Mr. Bright
and his followers may hold a place in political England as
usefully as the drunken Helots did in the social usages of
Sparta.   But though we have no great zeal for the con-
version of the Abbot of Unreason and his motley followers,
we think the country will agree with us that they ought
not to be taken by the hand by those in high places, and
allowed to play their pranks in the government of the
country.'   (*Blackwood's Edinburgh Magazine*, Vol. XCIII,
pp. 247–49).

As indicative of the feeling of instinctive apprehension, not to say vague dread, with which the rise
of the new Democracy was regarded in the middle
Victorian period, the following from the correspondence of the Prince Consort is significant.   Referring
to a talk with Lord Derby, then Premier, in March
1852, the Prince noted a remark of Derby's to the
effect that the 'leading Whigs were very much dissatisfied with the company they found themselves
thrown into, and alarmed at the progress of Democracy'.   And nine months later the Prince again
noted with evident satisfaction a further assurance
from the same source that the Tory leader, then about
to resign, ' was ready to support as far as he could,
any administration which was sincerely anxious to

check the growth of Democracy.' (*Queen Victoria's Letters*, Vol. II, pp. 66, 500.)

Sixty years afterwards this 'Democracy' was defined by the Duke of Northumberland in debate in the Lords as 'simply that kind of government which invariably prevails in one form or another in the decay of a State'. (House of Lords, May 16, 1911.)

I
PRINCIPIA

I

PRINCIPIA

Such of you as chance to be more careful newspaper readers may not improbably have noticed within the last few days a series of cable messages from America relating to a difficulty now assuming a shape more or less ominous of trouble between the United States and Japan. Actuated by a strong racial prejudice, and, as they assert, moral and other considerations, the Legislature of the State of California is considering, and seems about to enact, some very drastic measures of legislation generally anti-Asiatic in character, but in their operation distinctly aimed at immigration from Japan. This State legislation, it is alleged, is in manifest contravention of our treaty obligations with Japan, and may, if passed, involve the national Government in serious Eastern complications. The action referred to is taken under cover and by virtue of what we in America know as State Sovereignty; and those who have followed the course of events as day by day developed in the cable dispatches may have noticed, not perhaps without surprise and even a sense of bewilderment, that our newly elected President, just installed in his high office, is greatly perturbed over the outlook. To such a degree indeed is he perturbed that he has not only addressed a formal remonstrance to the California State authorities against the passage of the enactments in question, but he, head of the nation, is about to send his newly appointed Secretary of State—the first member of his Cabinet—across the continent to secure at least a modification, should the enactment of some legislation of the character referred to be insisted upon. Certainly, this is a most unusual proceeding—a proceeding indeed wholly unprecedented in American annals, and to foreign nations altogether incomprehensible. On the other hand, the dispatches tell us that the entire State of California is in arms against the Japanese settlers, the sentiment being general that they should be driven out. The President also is, we are assured by the same authority, advised that the anti-American feeling in Japan is growing rapidly, and that Japan considers the issue presented one of national honour.[1]

Here is a new international complication, involving not impossibly serious social issues. It arises out of the exercise of what we in America know as the power

---

[1] The situation at the close of the month of April, 1913, was as above set forth. Subsequently, the mission of Mr. Bryan, the Secretary of State, proved futile. The Californian Legislature insisted upon the passage of the enactments proposed, without modification; and the measure received the signature of the Governor of the State, regardless of the remonstrances of the President expressed through the Secretary of State. Public meetings denunciatory of this legislation, and indicating a strong popular feeling, were subsequently held at Tokio and elsewhere in Japan. A diplomatic correspondence ensued, with a request on the part of Japan that the point at issue be referred to arbitration. At this time (July, 1913) no definite agreement has been reached.

of State Sovereignty. With the issue thus presented as an international complication, I here and now have nothing to do; there is, however, from the historic point of view, much to be said on State Sovereignty as it exists as part of the United States governmental system. This is germane to my course, and the present is a very opportune time to enlarge upon it; for one of the leading London journals was the other day not far from the truth when it editorially said: 'Mr. Woodrow Wilson has not been long in discovering that doctrines that seem excellent in theory are often inconvenient in practice. One of the first requisites of the democratic faith is the sovereignty of the separate States of the Union. It has always been the tradition of the party to which President Wilson belongs to resist any extension of the authority of the Federal Government.' The topic here alluded to, if properly handled, while not without its dramatic features, has a decided historical interest. I now address myself to it; it involves the growth of a people, the crystallization of a nationality.

From its inception in the earliest stages of your own Great Rebellion, to its consummation in the outcome of our Civil War, this growth in the case of the United States covered a period of approximately two hundred years. It is not my purpose, neither indeed, in the time at my disposal, would it be possible, to enter in any detail into the history either of the entire period or of the later struggle, to which I have just referred, which closed it; and, moreover, that later and final struggle has recently been sufficiently here traversed [1] by another more competent than I. My plan, therefore, is to deal in this course only with certain phases of the general history and the more recent conflict, or some aspects of both which hitherto have either wholly escaped the notice of the historian or have in my opinion been insufficiently dealt with.

Historical parallels and generalizations are things dangerous to indulge in ; often deceptive, they are always open to criticism. With us of the English-speaking race, however, that date, the year of grace 1642 and the seventeenth of the reign of Charles I, challenges both parallelism and generalization ; it was, in short, epochal. For, in the closing half of 1642 and in the early months of the year next ensuing, began on both sides of the Atlantic concurrent and interacting processes, slow of movement at times and at times rapid, which in America worked to a final result in April, 1865, and which in Great Britain are to-day producing changes as pronounced as they are unmistakable—in fact, revolutionary. Witness your so-called Parliament Act of 1911. In America a Nationality resulted ; in Great Britain, Democracy.

Let me particularize. It was in June, 1642, that supremacy in the State was first claimed by Parliament—the Long Parliament. Practically, sovereignty was then assumed, it might be said arrogated to itself, by the House of Commons ; for the proclamation of King Charles, forbidding the muster of the militia,

---

[1] *Lectures on the American Civil War*, delivered before the University of Oxford in the Easter and Trinity Terms, 1912. By James Ford Rhodes. The Macmillan Company, 1913.

was then answered by a formal parliamentary declaration, carrying the stamp of royal authority, although his Majesty in his proper person might, as he did, disavow and oppose the same. A month later the first blood of Civil War—the War of the Commonwealth—was shed at Manchester; and on the 22nd of the following month the staff from which the royal standard flew was fixed in the ground here in Oxford, under circumstances so picturesquely described in Clarendon's stately narrative. In the language of the last and most thorough historian of the period, ' England was about to learn through suffering that wisdom which is to be found in neither of the opposing ranks.' From that day to this the lesson referred to has been wellnigh continuous. So far, England.

Meanwhile, on the other side of the Atlantic—our side—a more peaceful but not less momentous event was occurring. All through the latter months of 1642—the period following Edgehill in England—a confederation of the English settlements east of the Hudson river was under constant consideration. Finally, on May 19th, 1643, according to the calendar then in use—equivalent now to the 29th of the month—articles of union were signed by commissioners representing the colonies of the Massachusetts Bay, of Connecticut and of New Haven, in which the Plymouth Plantation joined in the following August. Entered upon under the hegemony of the Massachusetts Bay, ' it was the first example of coalition in colonial history, and constituted the germ that in the fruition of the following century became

the union of the States.' In other words, the step
taken May 29th, 1643, initiated a process finally
consummated on the 9th of April, 1865—Appomattox-
day, as we in America call it—that day on which
General Lee surrendered the Confederate Army of
Northern Virginia to the Army of the Union under
the command of General Grant.

Our American orators, historical writers, and
historians have since in all possible detail dealt with
periods and phases of this process, such as what is
known as our Revolutionary War—more properly,
the War of Independence—our Civil War, as they
have termed the War of Secession, or the framing of
our famous Federal Constitution; but these, one and
all, were merely incidents, or at most episodes in the
process of nation-building, which, begun in May, 1643,
closed in April, 1865. Subsequently to the first
Articles of Confederation, those of 1643, and prior to
the Federal Constitution of 1787, a succession of
attempts at closer or more comprehensive confederation were made—some theoretical and abortive, others
practical and operative—each marking an advance on
what went before, a striving towards the goal, an
aspiration to a fuller nationality; these, however,
were but phases of the process irresistibly, though for
long periods imperceptibly, proceeding. At first, and
for long, the movement was slow. At the close, it went
on with startling swiftness to the Appomattox climax.

Condensed, the story is one of absorbing interest;
and intelligently read it conveys also more than
one political lesson of general as well as practical

import—lessons, when properly studied, not without significance, possibly, to the England of to-day. I will endeavour briefly to summarize the process, avoiding details and yet trying to make clear what have ever seemed stumblingblocks or foolishness to those not to the manner born.

Every tolerably read Englishman or American is acquainted with Burke's famous vision of Lord Bathurst in his speech on conciliation with America. Burke there, you will remember, pictures 'the angel of this auspicious youth' opening to him a boyhood vision. The time was supposed to be 1714, the year of the death of Queen Anne, and the accession of King George I. Drawing the curtain which concealed the future, Burke's angel first unfolded the rising glories of England ; and while the youthful Bathurst 'was gazing with admiration on the then commercial grandeur of England', the genius, it is supposed, points out to him a little speck, scarce visible in the mass of the national interest, a small seminal principle, rather than a formed body, and in so doing, says : 'Young man, there is America—which at this day serves for little more than to amuse you with stories of savage men and uncouth manners ; yet shall, before you taste of death, show itself equal to the whole of that commerce which now attracts the envy of the world. Whatever England has been growing to by a progressive increase of improvement, brought in by varieties of people, by succession of civilizing conquests and civilizing settlements in a series of seventeen hundred years, you shall see as much added to her by

America in the course of a single life! If this state
of his country had been foretold to him, would it not
require all the sanguine credulity of youth, and all the
fervid glow of enthusiasm, to make him believe it?
Fortunate man, he has lived to see it!' Burke then
proceeds in another burst of rhetoric to call attention
to the fact that all this has been accomplished by 'a
people who are still, as it were, but in the gristle, and
not yet hardened into the bone of manhood. When I
contemplate these things,' he adds, ' when I know that
the colonies in general owe little or nothing to any care
of ours, and that they are not squeezed into this happy
form by the constraints of watchful and suspicious
government, but that through a wise and salutary
neglect, a generous nature has been suffered to take
her own way to perfection ; when I reflect upon these
effects, when I see how profitable they have been to
us, I feel all the pride of power sink, and all presumption in the wisdom of human contrivances melt and
die away within me. My rigour relents. I pardon
something to the spirit of liberty.'

If the long and memorable record of English parliamentary utterance, unique in history and educational
importance, contains a finer rhetorical outburst than
the foregoing, I can only say I am not acquainted
with it. This alone would justify quotation ; the passage is, however, also very opportune in the present
connexion. With that inimitable happiness of speech
peculiar to himself, Burke referred to the ' small
seminal principles' rather than 'formed bodies' dotted
in 1704 along the fifteen hundred miles of North

American Atlantic seaboard, which seventy years later, at the time Burke spoke, had by a process of natural growth become 'a people still, as it were, but in the gristle, and not yet hardened into the bone of manhood'. But the tropes and forms of speech in which he then clad his thought are to the American investigator of the present time curiously significant—they seem inspired. 'My pride of power sinks' . . . 'all presumption in the wisdom of human contrivance melts' . . . 'I pardon something to the spirit of liberty.' 'Power!', 'Human contrivances!', 'Spirit of liberty!' In these phrases was hidden the mystery of America's situation,—the problem of America's future, then matter of infinite question. Indeed, the chances of fate inclined distinctly towards disaster; for the spirit of liberty prevailed at that juncture in excess; 'power' was deficient; the 'human contrivances' essential to a successful solution of the problem remained to be devised. The situation, at best critical, was on any doctrine of chance fairly appalling. The question of man's capacity for self-government through representation based on general suffrage, was at issue. Would the provinces, freed from foreign guidance and motherly control, prove equal to the occasion?

As what ensued—that process of hardening from the 'gristle' of colonialism to the 'bone' of nationality—is familiar history, it will not here bear repetition; so I shall now condense volumes into a single page. The issue was two-fold: would the thirteen independent colonial offshoots develop among them leaders of the matured public spirit and constructive ability adequate for the work in hand to be done, that work being a practical scheme of centralized government? and, this leadership and constructive ability assumed, would the popular mass behind the leadership prove sufficiently advanced in political education to accept the results thus reached, and acquiesce therein? It was the old problem—Greece and the Achaian League over again, with two thousand years of human evolution intervening. What, if anything, had mankind learned in the interim? The world, and with cause, was very incredulous as to the answer this query was about to receive. Would an ordered nationality, or would a condition of chronic anarchy, emerge? The odds stood heavy in favour of the latter.

So far as leadership and constructive ability were concerned, the struggle for American independence had in its outcome been conclusive. They were there. Chatham, with the practised eye of a statesman—an eye both natural and trained—early recognized this fact, and bore witness of record to it. Such individualities as Washington and Franklin were conclusive as to leadership; while, as respects constructive ability, Massachusetts and Virginia took the lead. The latter evolved the Declaration of Independence; the former its written constitution of 1782, in the constructive aspect infinitely the more important production of the two. But, though the leadership was there, the question whether its teachings would not in practical working prove caviare to the general remained to be seen. Were the rank and file of those then inhabiting the thirteen provinces to be depended on to follow the leaders, and accept their conclusions? if not, those leaders were after all but voices crying in the wilderness. The world in such case would then but witness a repetition of Achaian experiences.

The ordeal was successfully met; but that final process of crystallization into a constitutional and confirmed nationality occupied close upon a century. Begun in 1776, it stood completed in 1865.

It was, and still is, fairly open to question whether the method of solving the problem adopted by the fathers in 1787 could not most fitly as well as accurately be described as a clever political trick, rather than an inspiration. It certainly would have been a trick, so far as the mass of those interested in the outcome were concerned, had the leaders in the constructive work then done themselves suspected what shape that outcome was to take. They most assuredly did not. Building better than they knew, they deceived themselves. They actually had faith in the metaphysical abstractions to which they had recourse! Time, outside pressure, and the rapid development of the resources of nature, then wholly undreamed of, did the rest. The study of what, step by step, occurred in the process is most interesting and, as respects the future, suggestive.

The obstacle in the way of crystallization lay in an excess of that 'spirit of liberty' to which Burke pronounced himself so tolerant; and in an absence of that 'power' to coerce in presence of which his pride

insensibly sank. The spirit of liberty in America, as
before in Greece, asserted itself in a pronounced cling-
ing to independence—local independence. An independence which bore a resemblance unpleasantly
suggestive of licence. Each one of the thirteen
original provinces asserted its sovereignty—loudly
proclaimed itself a nation. The provincialism was
intense; the mutual jealousies, dislikes, and aversions
only short of racial, were quite as pronounced as those
which formerly led to the downfall of the Achaian
League, or as more recently existed in the four
British nationalities; for Saxon never disliked or
despised Gael or Celt more than did Carolinians the
Yankee. As well attempt to crystallize oil and water!
Under such conditions the problem which taxed the
constructive ingenuity of the leaders, after the conflict
with Great Britain was over and outside pressure
withdrawn, was to devise a deception—a nationality
which should not be a sovereignty; and they actually
accomplished that feat, persuading others by first
thoroughly deceiving themselves.

To bring the result about they had recourse to what
I have already referred to as a metaphysical abstraction—they invented, what in perfect good faith
they proclaimed as divided sovereignty; but which
in reality was a most ingenious and deceptive
temporary *modus vivendi*. The proposition, in the
nature of a compromise, recommended itself to the
general popular mind; that compromises of this sort
are apt so to recommend themselves is matter of
common observation. The situation as then (1789)

existing in the general public understanding, North
and South, has been not unfairly stated in the
recent publication of a Confederate, still, half a century after Appomattox, quite 'unreconstructed', as we
phrase it; that is, a belated survivor of the 'Lost
Cause', one now in America occupying politically
much the position occupied here by a confirmed
Jacobite two centuries ago, or in France at present by
a dyed-in-the-wool Bourbonist.   Referring to our War
of Independence, the writer from whom I quote says:
'At no time during the rebellion [that is, the War of
Independence] did the American nations act as
a single nation.   A treaty was entered into by them
on November 15, 1777, the treaty being known as
Articles of Confederation. . . . This was the first
governmental union made by the American nations
for purposes other than war, and the object of this
union was to wage war successfully.   The nations
parties to the compact each continued to exercise full
powers of sovereignty; and, when they disapproved
any provision of the Confederation, such provision was
disregarded by them.'

Fired with that local spirit of liberty to which
Burke was so forgiving, this somewhat anarchistic
state of affairs seems yet to commend itself as ideal
to the judgement of this writer.   In other words, the
thirteen 'nations', which would now have increased
in number to forty-eight, then dwelt together in amity,
or otherwise, as the case might be, under a compact;
obeying the decrees of a central council when it was
agreeable for them so to do, and paying no attention

to them if not agreeable. Yet this writer, representing very fairly the liberty extremists, goes on to say that when the Federal Constitution was framed, 'Few of the American nations, if any, were willing to become parties to the written agreement until they had been assured that it should not be construed to affect their sovereignty in the least. They were willing to delegate specified powers to a holding company —such as the federal agents would make—for each nation would have the right to take back the powers so delegated.'

As I have said, this is the extreme States-right view of results brought about through the famous Federal Constitution of 1789. Historically, however, it can equally well be maintained that the Constitution was framed on the principle of a nationality—that is, Congress and the National Executive, as well as the State Legislature and the State Executive, acted directly on the citizen. Each having jurisdiction, the enactments and authority of each, within certain limits, applied to the individual, and he was thus subjected to a double or divided, and hence possibly conflicting, allegiance. The question, in fact, was whether the national powers thus delegated were irrevocable, or could at any time be recalled by the constituent State.

Such a system, which historically and beyond question was that which did exist in the early days of the Republic, constituted, though we were not conscious of the fact, a phase in a process of evolution—a transitory phase which might result in almost anything—segregation, consolidated nationality, not impossibly chronic anarchy. Meanwhile as a transitory phase—a condition of, so to speak, unstable equilibrium—it was marked by continual dispute and ill-feeling. This was true at nearly all times, and in separate sections of the country at different times. For example, within ten years of the adoption of the Federal Constitution, the National Government, confronted by a supposed political emergency, undertook to assert its sovereignty through the passage of statutes known as the Alien and Sedition Laws. Though the wisdom of the legislation was questionable, that its enactment was within the province of any nationality possessing sovereignty would at once to-day be admitted. It was, however, immediately and peremptorily challenged by the party of States-rights, Thomas Jefferson himself drawing up votes of nullification passed by the Legislatures of three States. Those enactments are now known in history as the ' Kentucky Resolutions of 1798 '. Thus early was foreshadowed the secession ordinances of sixty years later. Again, early in the following century the adherents of Jefferson, now President, being in political control, the four States then constituting the New England portion of the United States, disliking an embargo at that time imposed by the National Government in restraint of foreign commerce, gravely considered a withdrawal from the Union, though no overt act to that end was actually committed. As then presented, the issue was based exclusively on commercial considerations. A few years later, in 1820, the slavery question came to the front, there to remain until actual battle was joined; and, in the angry discussion which arose in connexion with new States about to be organized, threats of disunion through secession were freely made. The tariff was next the source of sectional strife, a system of agriculture based on slavery being the underlying cause of trouble. In this case one of the States—South Carolina—undertook to 'nullify', as it was termed, an enactment of Congress, declaring it inoperative within South Carolina's boundaries. The National Government was set at open defiance. This time the issue was compromised and temporarily adjourned, only presently to assert itself anew, slavery being again the underlying cause, primarily in connexion with the annexation to the United States of Texas, an independent republic. And now, once more, the State of Massachusetts, again committing no overt act, pronounced the violation of the Constitution so gross that a secession from the Union, though not actually attempted, might be considered justifiable. From this time on, and for fifteen years, slavery was continually at issue, with the menace of disunion for ever impending. A withdrawal was widely and loudly advocated at the South by the believers in an industrial system based on African slave labour; while in the North a peaceable dissolution was urged on the ground that, because of its recognition of slavery, the Federal Constitution was a compact with hell.

If ever a topic of contention was thoroughly thrashed out—so thrashed out, in fact, as to offer no possible gleaning of novelty—it might be inferred that among us in America this Divided Sovereignty conception had been subjected to that process. Yet years ago I ventured the opinion that such was not altogether the case; and to that opinion I still adhere. To my mind, the difficulty with the discussion has always been that throughout, extending as it has over the lives of three generations, it has in essence been too abstract, legal and technical—in a word, academic— and not sufficiently historical, sociological and psychological; in another word, human. It has been made to turn on the wording of certain written instruments. Yet those instruments were in themselves confessedly not explicit; and, when discussing them, far too little regard was paid to traditions, local ties, and inherited prejudices. As matter of fact, however, actual men as they live, move, and have their being, care little for acts of parliaments or theories, but they are the creatures of heredity: respecting local attachments, they yield obedience to custom. Especially is this true of those of the Anglo-Saxon breed; and it hence ensued that when the American Federal Constitution was framed, and a year later adopted—that is, in 1787–89—the dangerous question of ultimate sovereignty was instinctively avoided—treated as if its settlement was in no way imperative. The Federal Constitution, consequently, was both theoretically and avowedly based on a metaphysical abstraction—the idea of a divided sovereignty—in utter disregard of the fact that, when a final issue is presented—when, so to speak, the push-of-pike comes—sovereignty does not admit of division. It then rests in might. It always has so rested; and, in the nature of things, there rest it always must.

Yet even this last proposition, basic as it is, I have frequently heard denied. It is in argument replied that, as matter of fact, sovereignty is divided, and almost habitually divided—divided in family life, divided in the apportionment of the functions of government. Those thus arguing, however, do so confusedly. They confound sovereignty with an agreed, but artificial, *modus vivendi*. The Constitution of the United States, was, in fact, just that—a *modus vivendi*; ingenious, unquestionably, but still a *modus vivendi*. Under the circumstances, it was a most happy expedient for overcoming an obstacle in the way of nationality, otherwise insurmountable. To accomplish the end they had in view, the framers, deceiving themselves, had recourse to a highly deceptive device, under which it was left to time and the individual to decide, when the final issue should arise, if it ever did arise—and they all devoutly hoped it never would arise—where sovereignty, and consequently allegiance, lay. From the historical point of view there is indeed nothing in connexion with the history of American development more interesting than the growth and gradual evolution of this spirit of federal nationality. Slowly and imperceptibly supplanting State pride, it finally carried with it, as it inevitably must, sovereignty and allegiance. The process and outcome were long treated in a purely legal and technical way—it was a question of the verbal construction of an instrument. I, in all confidence, maintain that it was in reality at once a practical issue and an historical sequence. Treated as a practical issue, and not as a merely technical point in controversy, it was in the course of American history decided, and, moreover, correctly decided, both ways at different times in different sections, and, at different times, in opposite ways in the same section.

This sounds paradoxical — to the Confederate a stumblingblock, to the European foolishness. And yet the case is necessarily as stated. For, as development progressed on various lines in different times and localities, the sense of allegiance shifted. Two whole generations passed away between the adoption of the Federal Constitution in 1789 and the War of Secession in 1861. When that war broke out, the last of the framers of the Constitution had been a score of years in his grave. Evidence, however, is conclusive that, until the decennium between 1830 and 1840, the belief was nearly universal that in case of a final, unavoidable issue, sovereignty resided in the State, and to the State its citizens' allegiance was due.

The technical argument—the logic of the proposition — seems plain ; in fact, unanswerable. The original sovereignty was indisputably in the State ; in order to establish a nationality certain attributes of sovereignty were ceded by the several States to a common central organization—what Jefferson described as a Department of Foreign Affairs; all attributes not thus specifically conceded were reserved to the States ; and no attributes of moment were to be included by construction. Yet no attribute is so important as allegiance, citizenship. So far all is elementary, indisputable. And now we come to the crux of the proposition. Not only was all allegiance—the right to define and establish citizenship—not among the attributes specifically conceded by the several States to the central nationality, but, on the contrary, it was explicitly reserved. The instrument definitely declared that 'the citizens of each State' should be entitled to 'all Privileges and Immunities of Citizens in the several States'. This, and, as respects citizenship, nothing more. Ultimate allegiance was, therefore, due to the State which defined and conferred citizenship, not to the central organization which accepted as citizens whomsoever a State pronounced to be such.

Thus far the situation is historical; nor does there seem any escape from the logical deduction to be drawn from it. Citizenship, originating with the several States, of course involved allegiance to the State. But, speaking historically, and in a philosophical rather than a legal spirit, it is little more than a commonplace to assert that one great safeguard of the Anglo-Saxon race—what might almost be termed its political palladium—has ever been that hard, if at times illogical, common-sense, which, recognizing established custom as a binding rule of action, found its embodiment in what we are wont with pride to term the Common Law. Now, just as there can, I think, be no question as to the source of our American citizenship, and, consequently, as to ultimate sovereignty when in 1789 the Constitution was originally adopted, there can be equally little question that during the lives of the two succeeding generations a custom, so to speak, of nationality grew up which became the accepted Common Law of the land, and practically binding as such.[1] This was true in the South as well as the North, though the custom was more hardened into accepted law in the latter than in the former ; but the growth and acceptance as law of the custom of nationality even in the South were incontrovertibly shown in the very act of secession—the seceding States at once crystallizing into a Confederacy. Nationality in some form was assumed as a thing of course ; and Nationality must involve Allegiance.

But the metaphysical abstraction of a divided sovereignty, none the less, bridged a dangerous chasm. As a *modus vivendi* it did its work ; and did it well, because, finally, it worked into Might. Illogical, it was inevitably fraught with possible disputes and consequent dangers ; but it naturally came to pass that in many of the States a generation grew up, dating from the second of our wars with Great Britain—that known as the War of 1812—a generation which, gravitating steadily, and more and more strongly, to nationality, took an altogether different view of allegiance. Those of this generation were, moreover, wholly within their right. The sovereignty was confessedly divided ; and it was for those of the new generation to elect. The movements of both science and civilization were

[1] See note 1, p. 53.

behind the Nationalists. The railroad obliterated State lines, while it unified the nation. What did the foreign immigrants, now swarming across the ocean, care for States? They knew only the nation which adopted and protected them. Brought up in Europe, the talk of State Sovereignty was to them foolishness. Its alphabet even was incomprehensible. In a word, it, too, was 'caviare to the general'.

Then the issue, from the beginning inevitable, at last arose; arose over African slavery. Slavery was sectional. Because of it, as a domestic institution of theirs, the States south of a given line were arrayed against the States north of that line. Owing largely to slavery, and the practical exclusion of foreign immigrants because thereof, the States of the South had never undergone nationalization at all to the extent those of the North had undergone it. The growing influence and power of the National Government, the sentiment inspired by the wars in which the nation had been engaged, the rapidly improving means of communication and intercourse, had produced their effect in the South; but in degree far less than in the North. Thus the curious result was brought about that when, at last, the long-deferred issue confronted the country, and the *modus vivendi* of two generations was brought to a close, those who believed in national sovereignty—the North—constituted the conservative majority, striving for the preservation of what then was, the existing nineteenth-century Nation; while those who passionately adhered to State Sovereignty—the South—treading in the footsteps of the fathers, had become eighteenth-century reactionists. Legally, each had right on his side. The theory of a divided sovereignty had worked itself out to its logical consequence. 'Under which king, Bezonian?' —and every man had to 'speak or die'.

In the North the situation was simple. State and Nation stood together. The question of allegiance did not present itself, for the two sovereignties were merged —the greater had, by a natural process, absorbed the less. It was otherwise in the South; and there the question became, not legal or constitutional, but sentimental and practical. The life of the nation had endured so long, the ties and ligaments had become so numerous and interwoven, that, all theories to the contrary notwithstanding, a peaceable secession from the Union—the actual exercise of State Sovereignty —had become impossible. If those composing the several dissatisfied communities would only keep their tempers under restraint, and exercise an almost unlimited patience, a theoretical divided sovereignty, maintained through the agency and intervention of the Supreme Court—in other words, the perpetuation of the *modus vivendi*—was altogether practicable; and probably this was what the framers had in mind under such a contingency as had now arisen. But that, after seventy years of union and nationalization, a peaceable and friendly taking to pieces was possible, is now, as then it was, scarcely thinkable. Certainly, with a most vivid recollection of the state of sectional feeling which then existed, I do not believe there was in 1861 a man in the United States—I am confident there was not a woman in the South—who fostered self-delusion to the extent of believing that the change was to come about without a recourse to force. In other words, practical secession was revolution theoretically legal. Why waste time and breath in discussion! The situation became manifestly impossible of continuance when the issue between heated men, with weapons handy, was over a metaphysical distinction involving vast material and moral consequences.

Historically, such were the conditions to which natural processes of development had brought the common country at the mid-decennium of the century. People had to elect; the *modus vivendi* was at an end. Was the State sovereign? or was the Nation sovereign? And it thus came about that when, in that stormy April of 1861, the cry at last went forth, ' To your tents, O Israel! ' it mattered not at all whether the issue over which battle was joined loomed large or seemed small—whether it was a straw or an empire, an abstraction or the servitude of a race. In point of fact, Burke's 'little specks scarce visible,' those ' small seminal principles rather than formed bodies ' of 1714, had assumed organic shape; the long period of gestation was over; it was the final birth-throe of a perfected nationality. And yet foreign communities —you here in Great Britain—watched the tragedy in bewildered amazement, innocently asking what it was all about anyhow, and did it signify anything!

In this, the first lecture of my course, I have thus attempted to deal with the growth of Nationality in

the United States; but, obviously, the query at once
suggests itself, if this is so, and, as the outcome of the
Civil War, nationality stands established, how explain
the position of California, referred to in my opening?
How can a State, no longer sovereign, legislate in
contravention of the treaty obligations of the nationality of which it is a part? A contradiction in terms
is implied. The answer is, however, simple. State
Sovereignty exists still in theory, but it is no longer
accompanied by the claim to any right of its enforce-
ment through secession. That issue was fought out,
and, in 1865, decided for all time to come. State
Sovereignty in America is now admittedly limited to
an arbitrament by a final judicial tribunal — the
Supreme Court of the United States passing, and
passing without a right of further appeal, on any
concrete issue which may be raised by an Act of local
legislation. Under our written Constitution, treaties
entered into by the National Government with foreign
powers are the supreme law of the land, overriding all
contravening domestic enactments. State Sovereignty
is thus strictly limited; nationality has superseded it.
It is obvious and undeniable that serious complications, both domestic and involving foreign nations,
may in future arise from this somewhat anomalous
feature in our political system — a feature which
foreigners find it so difficult to understand, involving
as it does an *imperium in imperio*. Into that branch of
the subject I do not here enter; though it too has its
history, and of it I shall have more to say on a future
occasion. Now, I confine myself to a narrative sketch

of the origin of State Sovereignty in our system; to a brief reference to its logical outcome; and, finally, to a statement of the limitation placed upon it by the development of nationality recognized as supremely sovereign. A clear grasp of these fundamental propositions and their historical development is necessary to any intelligent comprehension of American history. With us, as with Great Britain, it has all been a process of slow growth; and in no respect an extemporized and ingenious invention.

In my next, or second, lecture I shall describe what my own investigation has led me to consider the crisis in the fierce struggle at the close of a two-century process—that inner impulse which then rent the veil of the old husk—the deciding battle of underlying antagonistic forces. The field of that battle was not, as I see it, at Washington, or at Gettysburg, nor indeed in America at all; it was here in England— here in your Lancashire cotton-spinning district and in Downing Street. About it too there was something Homeric. A struggle, not of arms but of industry and ideals; it was decided on no vulgar field of fight. In it the Confederacy sustained what proved, in the end, its fatal overthrow; and in it figured historical characters very familiar to English ears— Palmerston and Cobden, Bright and Gladstone, Napoleon III and Abraham Lincoln. Great forces were also there aligned—forces moral as well as material, of which history must now take cognizance and with them reckon. Taken altogether and viewed in a half century's perspective, though as yet unnoticed by any historian with whose pages I am familiar, my topic for next Wednesday constitutes an episode in nineteenth-century history than which none is either more dramatic or more pregnant with consequences of world-wide future significance.

NOTE 1, PAGE 47.

The question of national citizenship under the Federal Constitution, and irrespective of the States, is interesting, and, in the course of adjudication, has been much discussed. It was finally provided for by the passage of the Fourteenth Amendment to the Federal Constitution, one of the sequences of the Civil War, adopted in 1868. Prior to the incorporation of that amendment, there was no constitutional, much less any statutory, provision covering the case; and if national citizenship, apart from citizenship of a State, existed at all, and it undoubtedly did exist, it could only have been through custom meeting an exigency, and hardening into common, or judge-made, law. On this point a high, though lay, authority has recently thus expressed himself :—

It may, however, be said that those who totally deny the possession by the United States of any common law would confer a favour upon us if they would indicate from what other source citizenship of the United States by birth was, prior to the Fourteenth Amendment, universally derived. Citizenship by naturalization was a constitutional status, for Congress was expressly authorized to prescribe a uniform rule of naturalization; but prior to the Fourteenth Amendment, which declared 'all persons born . . . in the United States, and subject to the jurisdiction thereof ', to be ' citizens of the United States', there was no constitutional definition of national citizenship by birth. Mr. Justice Curtis, in his dissenting opinion in the Dred Scott case, argued that the Constitution adopted as native American citizens such persons as were by birth 'citizens' of the several States; but this theory failed to account for the fact that persons born on territory within the jurisdiction of the United States, but not within the jurisdiction of any State, were also regarded as citizens of the United States. We seem indeed to be driven to accept as correct the declaration of the Supreme Court, in 1898 (*United States v. Wong Kim Ark*, 169 U. S. 649, 675), that 'beyond doubt' birth 'within the sovereignty of the United States' created, by virtue of the rule of the common law operating thereunder, national citizenship. John Bassett Moore, *Four Phases of American Development* (1912), pp. 58-9.

II

THE CONFEDERATE COTTON CAMPAIGN

LANCASHIRE, 1861–1862

THE CONFEDERATE COTTON CAMPAIGN

LANCASHIRE, 1861–1862

GENERAL FRIEDRICH VON BERNHARDI is a distinguished Prussian army officer, ranking high as a military authority. As such he not long ago published a volume which, translated into English, has excited notice, and some newspaper and other criticisms. Written ' out of the fullness of my Germanic heart ', as the author asseverates, it records matured convictions. With those convictions—almost needless to say bellicose in the extreme—I here have nothing to do; but in the volume I find two historical references which afford what may serve as a text for this the second lecture of my course. In Chapter V of General Bernhardi's work, a chapter entitled ' World-Power or Downfall ', is the following : ' Since England committed the unpardonable blunder, from her point of view, of not supporting the Southern States in the American War of Secession, a rival to England's world-wide Empire has appeared on the other side of the Atlantic in the form of the United States of North America, which are a grave menace to England's fortunes. The keenest competition conceivable now exists between the two countries.'

Again, in a subsequent chapter (XII), a chapter entitled 'Preparation for the Next War', General Bernhardi reverts to this topic, once more forcibly recording therein his 'Germanic heart' conviction. Referring to Germany's present naval policy, and what he terms 'peace and renunciation', he here says: 'This policy somewhat resembles the supineness for which England has herself to blame, when she refused her assistance to the Southern States in the American War of Secession, and thus allowed a power to arise in the form of the United States of North America which already, although barely fifty years have elapsed, threatens England's own position as a World-Power.'

That the struggle which this author designates, and in my opinion very correctly designates, as the American War of Secession—more commonly by us in America called the Civil War, as if no other civil war had ever been waged—that this struggle, covering in American history the four years between April 1861 and April 1865, does not loom up in such large proportions in the British memory as in ours I am well aware. Here in Great Britain now practically forgotten, at the time, as I had occasion to observe in my previous lecture, its developments were watched with the deepest interest by all classes. They excited an intensity of feeling at present not easy to realize. The entire community was in fact divided into partisans of one side of the conflict or of the other, the cause of the Confederacy enlisting in its support a large preponderance of those then constituting what were known as the English governing classes.

This, however, was fifty years ago, and the generation which, observing the conflict thus divided over it, has passed from the stage. Other and equally momentous struggles more immediately affecting British interests and much nearer home— the Franco-Prussian War of 1870, with its capitulation of Sedan and siege of Paris; the Russo-Turkish War of 1877, with its story of Plevna; your South African War of 1898; the Russo-Japanese War of 1905—all these have since occurred, each for the time engrossing attention. So far as our Civil War of half a century ago is concerned, these I am well aware have operated on the public memory here much as a succession of tides on the sands of one of your ocean beaches. Through their action and agency previous footprints have been effaced.

It is apt to be so; and yet this rule also has its exceptions. Take, for instance, the so-called Wars of Napoleon—the life-and-death struggle which, following the outbreak of the French Revolution, lasted almost continuously from 1792 to 1815; in spite of all that has since occurred, that conflict of peoples and of giants, looming ever larger in history, dominates the literature of to-day.

I am, therefore, by no means prepared here to suggest that our American Civil War, however considerable in its proportions or momentous in results, exceeded in its tragic elements or equalled in historic significance other experiences of the last century, much less those of all recorded times. Occurring fifty years since, as respects the dramatic element,

while, as I shall presently show, by no means devoid
thereof and that in a large way, it will in no wise
bear comparison with another and earlier experience
—the Napoleonic drama, working rapidly out of its
tragic Russian phase to its close at Waterloo exactly
a century ago.

And yet premising all this, here is a German utterance of to-day referring to our struggle as one of
world-moment, characterizing the British policy
then pursued as an 'unpardonable blunder' involving
to-day 'grave menaces' to England's fortunes, even
threatening England's position as a 'World-Power'.
And this utterance suggests material more than
sufficient for an hour's discourse. So to-day I propose
to recall the events of a most critical as well as dramatic situation, and to lay bare, if I can, the hidden
motives which then influenced, and in the end
controlled, the momentous policy pursued by the
British Government. An interesting as well as
highly suggestive page of history, it is as yet un-
handled in any narrative.

To make plain the situation it is necessary to refer
in a certain detail to events and personages now in
a great degree forgotten, but which, recalled, still
possess interest.

At the close of my last lecture, it will be remembered, I referred to the formal secession from the
American Union of eleven of the States so-called
sovereign, and their organization into a new nationality calling itself the Confederate States of America.
This occurred during the winter and spring months

of 1861, and led to an immediate outbreak of hostilities between the two organizations—the Union, con-
sisting of the States which remained loyal to the
National Government, and, on the other hand, the
Confederacy. The issue of nationality was thus at last
squarely presented : it was, as I said in my last
lecture, more, far more, than a question of constitutional law and the construction either in language or
in spirit to be given to any parchment. Immediate
material results, or even the question of human servitude, were in the conflict ensuing minor considerations.
What was then in process, as I a week ago pointed
out, far transcended all this—it was in fact the final
birth-throe which preceded the appearance on this
planet of a consolidated nationality—a new World-
Power of the first magnitude.

It is proverbially easy to be wise after the event ;
and to the modern investigator, especially if European,
the cause of the American Civil War is now deemed
obvious ; and, in view of the immense preponderance
of strength and resources—men, money, munitions—
indisputably, and from the beginning, enjoyed by one
of the parties in the strife, its outcome was inevitable.
These discrepancies considered, the only real occasion
for surprise, it is now alleged, was that the weaker
party ever challenged the conflict ; and the conclusion
finally reached is that, under the circumstances, the
length to which the hopeless conflict was protracted
was not over and above creditable to the party finally
triumphant.

With a plausible sound, this is a very shallow

generalization. Nor is it in accordance with facts; for it so chanced that in 1861, when the slowly gathering tempest broke, a census of the entire United States had just been taken, and every figure now open to the investigator was then published. The public men and journalists of the South had studied the tables of the census; Europe had free access to them. And yet in the spring of 1861 and during three of the four years of following strife, no Southern man felt a doubt as to the final result, and no unprejudiced observer anywhere believed that the subjugation of the Confederacy was probable. The restoration of the old Union was considered, humanly speaking, an impossibility. The Confederacy numbered eight millions. No community numbering eight millions as well organized and combative as the Confederacy, ever yet had been overcome in the outcome of a civil war, nor was there any sufficient reason for supposing that the present case would prove an exception to a rule hitherto without exceptions. Such was the belief currently entertained. Moreover, it is a well-established historical fact that every single representative of a foreign nation then resident in Washington, in 1861 and 1862 regarded the division of the American Union as practically accomplished; they all took for granted the conclusion later expressed by Mr. Gladstone, that the success of the Southern States, so far as regarded their separation from the States of the North, was an event as certain as any event yet future and contingent could be.

Neither is it true that the outcome of the struggle

was from its commencement inevitable. On the contrary, I with confidence maintain that the result was in the beginning to the last degree doubtful; and, indeed, throughout the entire first half of the conflict—that is, until the summer of 1863—the chances largely favoured the Confederacy. Finally, its failure was due to contingencies not possible to forecast, and against which no human sagacity could have provided.

In the first place, as respects the cause of the conflict and the parties to it. And here I must severely condense. The slave-owning States constituted in 1860 a geographical section occupied by a community almost exclusively devoted to agricultural pursuits, and leading to a certain extent a patriarchal existence. Contented with their lot, they neither desired nor countenanced change. Intensely provincial, as is the wont of all agricultural and patriarchal communities, they looked upon the diversified industrial communities of the North, their partners in the common country, with a contempt they felt no call to conceal. Believing themselves to be in all respects a superior race, they were, moreover, persuaded that the world and its future were theirs. In view of what subsequently occurred this sounds absurd. I have no time in which to marshal evidence of the truth of what I have said; but listen to a few of their utterances. J. H. Hammond, an ex-Governor óf South Carolina, a Senator of the United States upon whom had fallen the mantle of Calhoun, was a representative Southern man. As such men went, he was thoughtful and observant. Writing in April preceding by a year the breaking out of the Civil War, Mr. Hammond thus expressed himself: 'I firmly believe that the slave-holding South is now the controlling power of the world; that no other power would face us in hostility. This will be demonstrated if we come to the ultimate. I have no wish to bring it about, yet I am perfectly ready if others do. There might be with us commotion for a time; but cotton, rice, tobacco and naval stores command the world; and we have sense enough to know it, and are sufficiently Teutonic to carry it out successfully. The North, without us, would be a motherless calf, bleating about, and die of mange and starvation.'

Thus the Confederacy did not go into the conflict of 1861 unadvisedly. On the contrary, its leaders gave what at the time they considered full consideration to all the factors on either side essential to success. They reckoned without their host; but, none the less, they did reckon. For instance, take the matter of the blockade, an inevitable incident to the struggle should it come about, and, finally, when it did come about, the controlling factor in its outcome. The very James H. Hammond, from a letter of whom I have just quoted, thus, in a speech delivered in the United States Senate Chamber in 1858, which I shall again have occasion to refer to, summarily and contemptuously dismissed as an absurdity the idea of an effective blockade of the Confederate coasts in case of war. He said: 'We have 3,000 miles of continental sea-shore line so indented with bays and crowded with islands that when their shore-lines are added, we have 12,000 miles . . . Can you hem in such a territory as that? You talk of putting up a wall of fire around 850,000 square miles so situated! How absurd!' As respects the undervaluation of the prospective opponent, the mental condition of the South in 1861 was well calculated to excite subsequent historic doubt; for, curious as it sounds in view of the ultimate outcome of the struggle, there is no exaggeration in the statement that in the first flush of war the masses of the South really believed that one Southerner 'could whip a half-dozen Yankees and not half try'.

As respects that factor of self-deception, the well-nigh inconceivable overvaluation of itself by the South as a commercial world-power, the mere mention of the delusion recalls to every American's memory the once familiar, now forgotten, postulate, ' Cotton is King!' Inconceivable, meaningless now to the European, to the South its infatuation on this point was in 1860 the fruitful mother of calamity; for the commercial supremacy of cotton, accepted as a fundamental truth, was made the basis of political action. The statement of the unquestioning faith in which that patriarchal community cherished this belief, now passed out of memory, savours of exaggeration. As a matter of fact, it does not admit of overstatement. For instance, what modern historical presentation could be so framed as to exceed in strength, broadness and colour the following from the speech just referred to as delivered, March 4, 1858, by James H. Hammond,

representing and voicing South Carolina. Senator
Hammond then said:—

But if there were no other reason why we should never
have war, would any sane nation make war on cotton?
Without firing a gun, without drawing a sword, should they
make war on us we could bring the whole world to our feet.
The South is perfectly competent to go on one, two, or three
years without planting a seed of cotton. . . . What would
happen if no cotton was furnished for three years? I will
not stop to depict what every one can imagine, but this
is certain: England would topple headlong and carry the
whole civilized world with her, save the South. No, you
dare not make war on cotton. No power on earth dares
to make war upon it. Cotton *is* King. Until lately the
Bank of England was king, but she tried to put her screws
as usual, the fall before the last, upon the cotton crop, and
was utterly vanquished. The last power has been conquered.
Who can doubt, that has looked at recent events, that cotton
is supreme? [1]

Thus, in complete provincialism and childlike faith,
a community was willing to venture, and actually
did venture, life, fortune and sacred honour on its
contempt for those composing the largest part of
the community of which they were themselves but
a minority. They staked their all on the soundness
of a commercial theory politically applied.

But perhaps the curious and complete state of
misapprehension, material and moral, then pervading
the Southern community has best been described by
a Southerner who himself at the time shared in it to
the full extent. Writing nearly fifty years later, he

[1] *Selections from the Letters and Speeches of James H. Hammond*
(New York, 1866), pp. 316, 317.

said: 'Two ideas, however, seemed [in 1861] to pervade all classes. One was that keystone dogma of secession, " Cotton is King!" the other that the war—did one come—could not last over three months. The man who ventured to dissent from either idea, back it by what logic he might, was looked upon as an idiot, if his disloyalty was not broadly hinted at.'[1]

Had the theory as respects the potency of cotton on which the South went into the war been sound, the blockade would have proved the Confederacy's most effective ally; for the blockade shut off from Europe its supply of cotton as it could have been shut off by no other possible agency. The Government of the Union in so far played the game of the Confederacy, and played it effectively. In the early days of the struggle, they even in their self-delusion talked at Richmond of an export duty on their one great staple, and of inhibiting its out-go altogether; but the blockade made quite unnecessary any action of that nature. Through the blockade the cotton-screw, so to speak, was applied to the fullest possible extent. Nor was the overthrow of the potentate easily brought about. Well entrenched, dethroning him entailed on the commercial world one of the most severe trials it has ever been called upon to pass through. Not all that Mr. Hammond predicted, or that the Confederate leaders confidently looked to see happen, actually did happen; but, none the less, the overthrow of the

[1] T. C. De Leon, *Belles, Beaux, and Brains of the '60's* (1907), p. 50.

Confederate Cotton idol involved a commercial and industrial disturbance of the first magnitude.

In addition to being titanic, it was also in the highest degree dramatic, for it involved nationalities, governments, and financial interests. All forgotten now, passed wholly from memory, it was at the time of a magnitude, interest and pathos not easy to exaggerate. It had in it an element of the Homeric; and, to the participants, it sometimes so appeared. Thus, for example, in glancing not long ago over a recently published biography of Mrs. Harriet Beecher Stowe, the author of *Uncle Tom's Cabin*, of which I shall presently have more to say, I came across this contemporaneous reference : ' Even the Greek mind never conceived a tragedy more terrible than the war between the States of North America.' This was not by Mrs. Stowe ; it is an extract from a letter written by a dying Confederate soldier to his mother from the field of battle. A young man about to enter the Presbyterian ministry, he had joined the army of the South in a true crusading spirit, and the whole tone of what he wrote breathed satisfaction that it had been given him to lay down his life for the cause of God and Truth as he saw it, as against injustice and oppression. The instance was not otherwise than typical.

Lancashire was the scene of conflict, and I have referred to the powers, potentates and principalities directly and indirectly participants in the battle there waged. Let me briefly marshal the two arrays. Here, alone, as you will presently see, is the material for an entire course of lectures, not one of which would be lacking in interest, especially in Oxford; and this I must compress into a few brief paragraphs. I will endeavour to do so.

In the assemblage of conflicting forces, those marshalled on behalf of the Confederacy vastly and in every respect preponderated; they did so, indeed, to a degree which now, viewed historically, should, judging by the test of all human experiences, have been conclusive of the outcome. It was suggestive of Pope's enumeration of the Homeric heavenly allies of Troy in his versified but most un-Homeric rendering of the *Iliad* :—

> In aid of Troy Minerva, Phoebus came,
> Mars fiery helmed, the laughter-loving dame,
> Zanthus, whose streams in golden currents flow,
> And the chaste goddess of the silver bow.

So now, in aid of the defiant, slave-holding Confederacy came, first, the great British and Continental commercial, financial, and cotton-spinning interests, with their far-reaching political influence; next, the suffering textile operatives, not only of Lancashire but wherever throughout other countries cotton was woven into cloth—they numbered millions; third, the entire governing classes, as they then were, of Great Britain, including the great landed interest. These last also were voiced, and most persistently as well as powerfully voiced, by the London *Times*, known as 'The Thunderer', at the acme of its great and memorable career. Finally, the French Emperor; for Napoleon III, now at the height of his prestige, for reasons of state to which I shall presently make brief reference, was disposed to put forth on behalf of the Confederacy all the influence he could exert. A powerful combination, it was one, in a worldly and political sense, wellnigh irresistible.

Opposed to it was an array so apparently meagre as to be almost pitiable; and if the alliance of forces I have just described recalled Homer, that set over against it was not less suggestive biblically—it was David again confronting Goliath. Strange, wellnigh inconceivable, when now asserted in the full light of the event, that opposing array consisted simply of John Bright, the Tribune in Great Britain of Political and Industrial Democracy, and behind him 'a little bit of a woman', as she at that time described herself, 'just as thin and dry as a pinch of snuff,' holding in her hand a book : but the woman was Harriet Beecher Stowe, and the book was entitled *Uncle Tom's Cabin; or, Life among the Lowly.*

As I make this statement—present that contrast— I know well enough not a few of those listening will smile in a spirit inwardly derisive. Setting it down to the account of exaggeration, they will dismiss my marshalling of forces as an attempt at the picturesque in speech. I none the less adhere to what I have said as a correct historic presentation ; and, did time permit, I would undertake to prove it such. But, for so doing, one lecture would not suffice ; four lectures might. In fewest words possible I will set forth the facts.

In contrasting the two arrays on that Lancashire field of battle, I enumerated five separate factors, each powerful, all working unitedly to promote the cause of the Confederacy. First, and most potent, among these were the British and Continental commercial, financial, and cotton-manufacturing interests. Upon them I need not dwell. Their all-pervading influence is too well known to make enlargement thereon needful. They represent the pocket nerve; and, when that is touched, as we all know, the system vibrates through all its parts. So let them pass.

Next came the textile operatives, the cotton spinners, whether of Lancashire or in France. With them it was a question of bread, rent and raiment; and on them the screws were put. In their case, cotton scarcity was synonymous with famine. The foreordained victims of that encounter, how would they, a mighty multitude, bear themselves in the cruel ordeal? We will presently see how they did bear themselves. Then followed the aristocracy and gentry of England; the landed and governmental interests of Great Britain and France. These, at that day the controlling factor in politics, were lined up almost solidly on behalf of the Confederacy. It was with them a matter of instinct quickened into action by self-interest; but, as your recent political outcome' has clearly shown, that instinct then inspired and impelled a class not less truly than on a well-known occasion the instinct of Sir John Falstaff acted, according to his own asseveration, in restraining his valour. Tennyson in his *Locksley Hall*, printed a score of years before, had prefigured it all—foreshadowed it on the Future's wall :

Slowly comes a hungry people, as a lion, creeping nigher,
Glares at one that nods and winks behind a slowly-dying fire.

The 'hungry people' in this case was simply Democracy, so phrased; and in 1862 the spectre Democracy was, in the English mind, typified in the trans-Atlantic English-speaking Republic. It was typified, too, in a way singularly contradictory. On the one side was a truly Democratic community, living under a republican form of government; and, on the other, developing itself in that same nationality, was a social and industrial organization with slavery as its admitted basis. That such a condition of affairs invited criticism was natural. That it had received it from English observers, travellers and writers—and that in a way which certainly did not lack in outspoken frankness—is matter of record; read now, for instance, Charles Dickens's *American Notes.* Meanwhile, a world-process plainly indicative of an advancing stage of moral development had been going on, not without its distinct manifestations in Great Britain. While the dislike and fear of Democracy were pronounced in one most influential portion of the community—the nobility and landed gentry, and upper-middle class—in those same classes, and yet more below in the great sleeping but seething mass of the community, the feeling against African slavery as it had existed in the West Indian Islands, and still did exist in the United States, had become a cult. True, among the more comfortably placed and materially well-to-do it had long since degenerated, as cults will, into a Pharisaic better-than-thou cant; but there was no question it still had a strong hold on the public mind and conscience.

This, however, notwithstanding, class feeling, class interests and social prestige overwhelmingly carried the day ; and it is susceptible of historic proof that in 1862 at least nine out of ten of those constituting the classes referred to, sympathizing with the Slave-holding Confederacy, exerted their whole influence to forward its interests.   They fully believed also that its success was assured.

Next in the array on the side of the Confederacy I have named 'The Thunderer'—the London *Times* newspaper of that mid-century period.   But here, on the threshold of a most tempting topic, I must hold my hand.   To that subject justice could not possibly be done in the fragment of an hour, and to that my time is limited.   Suffice it therefore to say that, now, the *Times* is a journal of very considerable influence ; but in comparison with what it was fifty years ago, and during our Civil War, it is but the shadow of its former self.   This topic, here summarized in a single paragraph, would in itself afford the material for an entire lecture, and a most interesting as well as instructive lecture ; one, too, not without its distinctly humorous side.

Never perhaps on this earth has any public organ occupied the position the *Times* held during the period referred to, or possessed the same journalistic power. In America especially 'The Thunderer' loomed very large ; and a carefully studied review of the policy as respects American affairs pursued by it during those eventful years—a review prepared without temper and in a purely judicial and investigating spirit—would constitute a truly valuable historical contribution, especially if seasoned with a restrained sarcasm and strictly subdued sense of the ridiculous. The language as respects American men and events then habitually indulged in on the *Times* editorial page seems now inconceivable; its arrogance knew no bounds, and the scorn it expressed for those of the Free States was limited only by its command of speech at once vituperative and contemptuous : we were a degenerate and insensate people—braggart, vulgar, sordid, corrupt and cowardly; blindly striving for an impossible result, in that we would persist in our attempt ' to conquer a nation, to escape whose victorious arms is the only triumph their [our] generals seemed capable of gaining'. Abraham Lincoln was the especial object of its disdain ; and as long ago as 1867 an English contributor to the *North American Review*, remarking on our misconceptions of English public men and events, philosophically and truly observed in conclusion : ' But they have never so misconceived a British statesman as, four years ago, we misconceived Mr. Lincoln, or gone so far astray in regard to any crisis of our history as we did in reference to the moving springs and results of their civil war.' And in this misconception and going astray ' The Thunderer' blazed and made broad the path. In wrong-headedness it fairly bore the palm.

Thus the *Times* was probably the most influential single factor in the formidable pro-Confederate array on that Lancashire field of battle. Its utterances, moreover, not only expressed what was passing in the minds

of its great and influential constituency, but to a large
extent foreshadowed during the year 1862 the Cabinet
action and foreign policy of Great Britain.   This, at
the time surmised, we now know.   Palmerston confi-
dentially inspired Delane.

The fourth and final factor in the strange combination I am describing was the French emperor—last
mentioned, in influence by no means least.   In 1862,
the period under consideration, Napoleon III was
at the climax of his imperial career.   Closing the
Crimean War by the Treaty of Paris in 1855, four
years later he had emerged from the Italian campaign
through the Peace of Villa Franca, if not in a blaze of
glory, at least with credit.   France posed as the
arbiter of Europe ; Great Britain was its ally.   Emperor
in fact as well as in name, no forecast of the fate not
remotely in store for his dynasty and for the country
he ruled had yet dawned on the somewhat grotesque
prisoner of Ham, much less was it imagined by the
world.   In appearance not less firmly fixed on the
imperial throne than his uncle after Tilsit, Louis
Napoleon was already entered on the first stage of that
policy which, eight years later, led to his downfall.
He had entered upon it also in a way which directly
involved him in American complications.

As we now know, Napoleon III was a dreamer,
a visionary ; but at the time with which I am dealing
he was not so considered.   Looked upon as a sagacious,
far-seeing political schemer, he had recently as a man
of action twice involved Europe in war ; and few
doubted his power or readiness again so to do if the

furtherance of hidden policies might thereby be
promoted. That the French taste for the grandiose
and scenic must periodically be gratified was moreover
fundamental in the Napoleonic legend. Accordingly
one of the somewhat Argonautic dreams in which the
Emperor indulged was that of a renewal of the French
trans-Atlantic dominion, lost in one region when in
1765 Wolfe scaled the heights of Quebec, and again
sacrificed in another for a mere mess of pottage when
in 1803 the first Napoleon made over the vast Louisiana domain to the United States. In 1861 the
occasion seemed opportune. The American political
waters were sorely troubled, and, angling in them,
Napoleon thought to please France by restoring to it
trans-Atlantic dominion under the guise of a Latin
sphere of French influence. And, curiously enough, in
this, historically adjudged the wildest and most visionary of his projects, Louis Napoleon did in fact but
anticipate a future not then remote. For in 1860 it is
to be remembered the Manchester School, so called,
was dominant in England politically, and the
Manchester School never wearied of preaching the
homely domestic virtues ; for a nation like an individual to stay at home and mind its own business, setting
an example in this respect to every other community,
was a cardinal article of Manchester faith. Accordingly the colonial systems and foreign spheres of
influence, now considered so necessary to national
development, were looked upon as burdens. Disraeli,
for instance, talked of our 'wretched dependencies',
and Gladstone accepted this idea to the extent that he

was willing in every way to facilitate the separation of the oversea British dependencies from the Mother Country. The extent to which the opposite policy now prevails need not be dwelt upon. That it is just as dangerous for a statesman to whom is entrusted the policy of a great empire to be in advance of the fad of the times as it is to be behind it, is a familiar commonplace. And thus it so chanced that Louis Napoleon, in the matter of oversea spheres of influence, was merely fifty years in advance of the age that now is.

Nevertheless, this policy, whether visionary or only premature, radically affected the views entertained by the French emperor as to American politics. The breaking up of the Union was essential to the success of his Mexican plans; and as I have already said, the cotton famine afforded most opportune occasion for the exercise of influence to that end. So the emperor thought to pose before France as the friend and benefactor of the idle and hungry operative. The efforts of the Imperial Government were, accordingly, now directed towards bringing about a joint intervention of Great Britain and France in our American conflict; which intervention could hardly have failed to result in a breaking of the blockade of the Confederacy seacoast, and the consequent division of the Union. The adoption of this policy by the Palmerston-Russell Government was the only thing necessary to success.

On the other hand, arrayed against the combination I have described, was simply one English public man, the recognized head of the dreaded and ever encroaching Democracy; and, as she portrayed herself in words

I have already quoted, 'a little bit of a woman . . . just as thin and dry as a pinch of snuff,' holding in her hand a printed book!

Of these, the oddly assorted champions of that momentous far-reaching combat, time again will not suffice to enable me adequately to speak; neither would it be right for an instant to suggest that John Bright was the single advocate in Great Britain of the combined cause of the African slave and American nationality. Others, some in the Ministry and even in the Cabinet—W. E. Forster, Milner Gibson, the Duke of Argyll—acted with him. Outspoken, whether in Parliament or Exeter Hall, were also Thomas Bayley Potter, the organizer of the Cobden Club; and, after the first few months of the struggle, Richard Cobden himself. With them were John Stuart Mill, Thomas Hughes, and, above all in University circles, Professor Goldwin Smith, then a comparatively young man. It is nevertheless, speaking within bounds, to say that, when it came to the working-man, the operative, John Bright at that time of crisis voiced the British Democracy at large. Like the *Times* with its constituency, he gave utterance to what was passing in the mind and breast of the wage-earner. Then at the acme of his great odium among those who constituted English social life, Bright had recently been characterized by Tennyson in *Maud,* his latest poem, and in every one's hands, as

This broad-brim'd hawker of holy things;

but he none the less, sympathizing with those of it, gave fearless utterance to the sentiments of the great, if otherwise largely inarticulate class in the community whose action in this particular contingency was to prove decisive of results. It is, therefore, only fair and historically reasonable to embody in the person and voice of John Bright that position I have assigned him. The English Gracchus, he was also the David in the forefront of the opposing Lancashire array.

I now, however, pass on to Mrs. Harriet Beecher Stowe and *Uncle Tom's Cabin*; and here again the time at my disposal is provokingly insufficient for any proper presentation of a topic singularly dramatic and altogether instructive : to those of the present generation, novel also. For, speaking generally, I think it may not unsafely be said that the book known as *Uncle Tom's Cabin*; *or Life among the Lowly*, published in 1852, exercised, largely from fortuitous circumstances, a more immediate, considerable and dramatic world-influence than any other book ever printed.

Superlatives are dangerous. I do not like them ; and I am conscious that I am now indulging in superlatives. Let me, therefore, call attention to the limitations here imposed. Mrs. Stowe's book, I say, exercised a more immediate, considerable and dramatic world-influence than any other book ever printed. I do not say that the influence referred to was more profound, subtle, lasting, or extensive. I do not think it was, even confining the comparison to contemporaneous publications. For instance, Darwin's *Origin of Species* appeared (1859) a few years only after *Uncle Tom's Cabin* (1852) ; and it has unquestionably exercised a far more profound and lasting influence : but that influence was neither so dramatic, nor so immediately considerable. And so of any other book which might be named. Upon this theme I now propose briefly to dilate.

In literature as in finance and business, in science and mechanics, everything depends upon appropriateness of time, place and condition. A word, like an invention, a discovery, or a person, must happen right. Coming at any other period, Peter the Hermit would have been a cowled crank, crying aloud from church steps a message to which no one gave ear. The world now is, as it always has been, full of such; but of them all Peter alone chanced exactly right. Rousseau was another case in point. His experience resembled more closely that of Mrs. Stowe; but the *Social Contract* (1762) preceded by thirty years that French Revolution it voiced, and which it so potently promoted. *La Nouvelle Héloïse* and *Emile* are, I fancy, not much read to-day, even in France; while I am informed that, in America at least, *Uncle Tom's Cabin* is still one of the books in greatest demand at the counters of our Public Libraries. And yet as a work of fiction I do not suppose that to-day Mrs. Stowe's story would be rated high; it was in no respect a literary masterpiece. Defective in construction, it was local in its incident, and, in its treatment, crude. No 'Uncle Tom' ever existed; and, moreover, had he existed, there would have been much truth in an observation attributed to Robert Toombs of Georgia. A leading Confederate notable—orator and politician—Mr. Toombs, while

wholly denying the actual incarnation ever of any
such African apostle and martyr to ideals as ' Uncle
Tom ', was accustomed to asseverate that, if such
an exemplar of the higher Christianity had existed
indeed, he would have furnished the most complete possible vindication of American African
slavery. What other industrial system or social
organization could point to a fetich-worshipping
Congo savage developed in three generations into an
altruistic saint? The tree is known by its fruits!
Nevertheless, all this to the contrary notwithstanding,
it so chanced that ' Uncle Tom ' hit the world, so to
speak, between wind and water. Composed at exactly the right time, it came out under conditions
which made possible its altogether exceptional vogue.
And in this connexion it is necessary to remember that in the mid-Victorian period the day of caste
was only just outlived ; and, so far as human servitude was concerned—that is, property in man—the
world had then newly reached a curiously responsive
stage. This was so not only in America but throughout Europe. Generally, mankind was asserting, or
ready to assert, man's claim for recognition as Man.
The word had only to be spoken ; and it chanced to
Harriet Beecher Stowe to speak it. The weak spot in
the system then prevailing, and which had prevailed
from the beginning, lay in African servitude in
America. Ethnological principles were not understood in 1850 as they now are ; those principles had
in fact not yet been reduced to a scientific basis.
While Darwin had not spoken, Mr. Disraeli oratoric-

ally arrayed himself 'on the side of the angels'.
Nevertheless, conditions were ripe, and circumstances
combined. So, to the utter amazement of Mrs. Stowe,
her book on its appearance was as a live ember
dropped in a field of dry stubble—almost as a torch
flung into a magazine of combustibles. Like the rising
of mighty winds, like the rushing of many waters,
almost immediately following the publication of the
story there came up from the earth a tumult of human
voices, expressing themselves in every known tongue.
Above all was the note of sympathetic weeping, and
the cry of those who said, 'Can nothing be done to
banish this accursed thing from off the face of the
earth?' Not only was *Uncle Tom's Cabin* universally
read, having been translated, it is said, into over twenty
foreign languages and sold by the million, but even
in those parts of it which challenged question and
inquiry it was taken so seriously and so accepted as
truth as to become a great political and moral force
throughout the world of thought and sentiment.
A sermon against a great moral evil, it was altogether
a homiletic exception, for it was a sermon every one
read. It was again curiously suggestive that after the
English sale of the book had run to over a hundred
thousand copies a reaction set in; and that reaction
was led off by the London *Times*. Yet, when a year
or two later Mrs. Stowe landed in Liverpool from the
steamer, she noticed a great throng gathered for some
reason on the dock. Was it always so on the arrival
of an American packet? It did not occur to that
particular Yankee 'school-marm' that the pier was

thronged with the plain people, eager to see her and
touch her raiment. It had never dawned upon her
that she was a person of importance ; and yet on the
occasion of her going out sight-seeing at Edinburgh
a few days later, she wrote : ' As I saw the way to
the cathedral blocked up by a throng of people that
had come out to see me, I could not help saying,
" What went ye out for to see : a reed shaken with
the wind ? " ' As she drove through Scotland the
butcher came out of his stall, the baker from his shop
to welcome her ; the miller dusty with flour, the bloom-
ing comely young mother with her baby in her arms,
bore witness, all smiling and bowing, with that
hearty, intelligent, friendly look as if they knew the
American authoress would be glad to see them, plain
people though they also were. When they instinctively greeted her as their friend, it was the chord of
universal and human tenderness she had struck so
opportunely in her book that was ringing in their
hearts. Then came the royal reception given her by
the Duke and Duchess of Sutherland at Stafford
House, where Lord Shaftesbury presented her on behalf of the women of England generally an address of
welcome and appreciation. It was the same everywhere on the Continent—in France, in Switzerland,
in Norway ; and when her subsequent book *Dred*
appeared, so inferior in character and interest that it
is now forgotten, one hundred thousand copies were
sold in four weeks. It is, however, unnecessary to
enter into further detail. As I have already said, it
would certainly be very difficult, I think it would be

impossible, to name any book ever published which led so immediately to such momentous consequences.

The opposing forces arrayed in Lancashire in 1862 were, therefore, not so altogether unevenly matched as would have been supposed. For John Bright, the Tribune of British Democracy, represented and gave voice to a great moral movement aroused to white heat by Harriet Beecher Stowe ten years before, and then moving onward with a world-momentum ever increasing.

To put it another way, so far as the formidable combination of interests advocating the cause of the Confederacy was concerned, the situation was suggestive of Browning's lines in his short and familiar lyric *Instans Tyrannus*:

> Do you see?   Just my vengeance complete,
> The man sprang to his feet,
> Stood erect, caught at God's skirts, and prayed !
> — So, *I* was afraid !

III

DIS ALITER VISUM

III

DIS ALITER VISUM

My last lecture came to a somewhat abrupt close. In it I had described the opposing arrays on the Lancashire field of conflict in 1862—that field selected by the leaders of the Confederacy. Staking their all on the issue there joined, they challenged a trial of strength. Cotton they had proclaimed King; and they were now prepared to demonstrate its world-sovereignty. Their confidence in the outcome was unquestioning; and of the opposing arrays theirs in every way distinctly preponderated.

In that terrible summer of 1862, the situation here as well as in America was in the highest degree dramatic; and, while with us the contending armies swayed to and fro in life-and-death grapple, what proved in the end the controlling decision was reached in England. But before a decision was reached, cotton unmistakably asserted its power. And that assertion of power, its intensity and the outcome of the effort put forth, is my theme to-day.

While well aware that the conditions then existing are now largely forgotten, I have neither time to enter into details, nor to attempt to recount, however briefly, a twice-told tale. I must assume a degree of general information. Suffice it then to say that, through the ingenuity of two Englishmen and one

American — Richard Arkwright, James Hargreaves, and Eli Whitney, the earliest of their inventions dating from about 1760—the weaving of cotton into cloth had a century later become one of the leading and most vital industries of the world; and, for reasons a knowledge of which must again be assumed, the States included in the Southern Confederacy enjoyed what they were fully convinced was an unshakable monopoly in the production of the indispensable staple. It was theirs through soil, climate, and an industrial system believed to be essential to its successful production. The complete dependence of this great and still rapidly expanding interest on one source for its supply of raw material had to the more far-sighted Englishmen long been occasion for solicitude; and, as early as 1847, John Bright had prophesied that an American industrial disturbance because of African slavery would some day seriously interfere with Lancashire's supply of raw material. As usual, no heed was given to the voice of warning; now, the contingency presented itself.

The American crop of 1860 had been the largest then recorded, aggregating nearly 4,000,000 bales. It had gone forward in the regular way, and, affording employment to a vast fleet of carriers, it fed innumerable looms. The foreign shipments—some 3,500,000 bales—were practically complete when in April, 1861, a blockade of the Confederate coast was suddenly declared by the Washington Government, following hard on the outbreak of active hostilities heralded by the bombardment and fall of Fort Sumter. A year later the supply of unmanufactured cotton in European ports was running ominously low; though the Confederate leaders loudly insisted upon it that the blockade was a mere paper fulmination, and that, so far as Confederate ports were concerned, both ingress and egress were practically unobstructed. The cotton shipment, they claimed, was withheld, to establish once for all Cotton World-mastery. In point of fact, while in May, 1861, the European supply of the staple was estimated at nearly 1,500,000 bales, during the same month a year later it had become reduced to a third of that amount. Liverpool then was, as it now is, the great cotton market of the world; and in Liverpool the stock had shrunk from close upon 1,000,000 to a little more than 360,000 bales; while the price per pound had risen from sevenpence to thirteen pence. The effect of the stoppage, to whatever cause due, was thus read in the market quotations; for, during the previous six months the quantity of cotton received from America had been hardly more than nominal—a mere 11,500 bales—while in the corresponding months of the previous year it had been 1,500,000 bales. In other words, the shipments for the half year ending in May, 1862, were less than one per cent. of the shipments during the same period of the previous year. The arm of industry was paralysed; and, throughout Lancashire, the distress already indisputably great was obviously increasing. One half of the spindles were idle; and, in the towns of Blackburn and Preston alone, over 20,000 persons were dependent on parochial aid. The newspapers teemed with pitiable cases of individual destitution; and the local strain on the poor laws was so severe that Parliament considered their modification. Meanwhile the period of six months, originally assigned by the Confederate economic authorities as the extreme limit of European endurance, was long exceeded. The pressure was great; the consequent suffering manifest. A further application of the screws would surely produce the desired effect. And, during the following months, the situation in the manufacturing districts under that freshly applied pressure grew rapidly worse, became in fact wellnigh unendurable. The looms which a year before had consumed on an average 40,000 bales of American cotton a week, now might count on receiving perhaps 4,000. On the other hand, the unprecedented price could not at once bring into the market anything even approaching an adequate supply from other countries. The receipts from Asiatic sources rose, for instance, from 174,000 bales in 1860 to nearly 700,000 in 1862 and close upon 900,000 a year later: but the staple was of inferior quality, and the Asiatic bale weighed materially less [10 per cent.] than the American. The real trouble, however, lay in the fact that the East India cotton as a manufacturing staple was at best a most unsatisfactory substitute for the American. Destructive to the machinery, it was hardly less hurtful to the hands and patience of the operative; and, while the spinners had been forced to buy the East India product, and adapt their machinery to it, yet the very first opportunity was seized to remit it again to the background. Experience confirmed prejudice, showing unmistakably that, unless the Indian staple were greatly improved, the demand for 'Surats', as it was denominated, would again fall to its former low estate.

And of this wholly artificial state of affairs the market quotations afforded convincing evidence. In May, 1862, American cotton ruled in Liverpool at thirteen pence per pound. It continued at about that price until July, when it rose to seventeen pence; and thence, in August, it crept on first to twenty pence, and afterwards by speculative leaps and bounds it went up and up until at last, on September 3, it was quoted at half a crown a pound. Under modern conditions, such figures were unheard of: but, a little later in the month even these figures were exceeded. The price of thirty-one pence a pound was recorded.

Cotton had thus become a speculative commodity. Too costly to manufacture into cloth at prices then ruling, and rapidly enhancing in value, it was, when not sold for export, held for yet further advance.[1] So by the end of September, out of 80,000 operatives in five localities in Lancashire only 14,000 were working full time, while the remaining 66,000 were about equally divided between those working on short time and those wholly idle. In twenty-four unions, 156,000 persons were represented as receiving poor relief; and yet the number was increasing at the rate of 1,000 per day. This was very bad;

[1] See Note 1, p. 122.

but, before the end of October, conditions were appreciably worse. In the same number of unions, 176,000 persons were receiving relief. In six succeeding weeks 35,000 persons had become paupers, while the wholly unemployed exceeded those working on full time by nearly two to one. An ex-Premier, the Earl of Derby, now speaking as Chairman of the Executive Committee of the General Relief Association, made the statement that at one period over 430,000 persons out of two millions, or nearly 22 per cent. of the whole population, were dependent 'for their daily existence either upon parochial relief or public charity'. The loss of wages for each working day was at the same time stated by Mr. Cobden to be in excess of £22,000.

Under such circumstances, the local resources, municipal and voluntary, were exhausted or manifestly inadequate for the work of necessary relief, and a call for aid went forth. Into the results of that call I have not time to enter. Suffice it to say all classes and the whole world responded. This, your University of Oxford, for instance, contributed £4,000 from its corporate funds. As the authoress of *Mary Barton*, not unfamiliar with previous periods of distress in the manufacturing districts, at the time expressed it, the supreme torture now applied was the one absorbing topic, 'literally haunting us in our sleep, as well as being the first thoughts in waking and the last at night.' Within thirteen months private charity provided nearly two millions sterling for the relief of distress ; but the loss of wages during the same period was computed by Mr. Gladstone as being in excess of £8,000,000.

The extraordinary fact in the situation was, however, the patience of the victims ; and the official organ of the Confederacy published in London, the *Index* newspaper, noted with surprise and unconcealed dismay the absence of political demonstrations to urge upon what it termed 'a neglectful Government' its duty towards its 'suffering subjects'.

A distinctly audible whine was perceptible in its utterances. One of them ran thus,—'It is the great peculiarity of England that the heart of the country is thoroughly religious ; ' and, speaking editorially, the writer then went on to assert that the prominence given to the slave question by American writers and preachers was hypocritical, and intended especially for the religious public in England. 'And well had it answered its purpose. To this very hour the great mass of the people have no other terms to express the nature of the conflict. It is to no purpose that argument, fact, and experience have shown the utter indifference of the North to the welfare of the negro ; the complete appreciation by the slaves themselves of the sham friendship offered them. . . . The emancipation of the negro from the slavery of Mrs. Beecher Stowe's heroes is the one idea of the millions of British who know no better, and do not care to know.' The fundamental sin of the Confederacy had in truth found it out. Literally, the curse of the bondsman was on it ; and perhaps never has there been witnessed in the history of mankind a more creditable exhibition of human sympathy, and what is known as altruism, than that then in Lancashire enacted. The common folk of a great English district, Abraham Lincoln's ' plain people ', workless, cold and hungry, felt, what the wealthier class refused to believe, that the cause at issue in America was the right of a working-man to his own share in the results of his toil, to the bread earned by the sweat of his brow. That cause, they instinctively knew, was somehow their cause ; and they would not betray it. So, no organized cry went up from suffering Lancashire to break the blockade which, while it shut up Cotton, was throttling Slavery. Touching evidence on this head, not without its comic features, was from time to time afforded. For instance, at the most intense period of distress, when the cotton-workers in Rochdale were starving in enforced idleness, a meeting was called in the town by a Liverpool association of Southern sympathizers, formed to promote the breaking of the blockade. The lecturer delivered his address ; and those composing the meeting then passed a resolution censuring him for endeavouring to mislead them !

The situation was suggestive of a closely beleaguered city—some modern Haarlem—representative of a common cause, one in which the entire community was heart and soul enlisted. This, one incident signally illustrated. When the Lancashire distress was most pronounced, news came there that sympathizers in the loyal portion of the American Union, though having at that juncture heavy burdens of their own to bear, yet felt moved to contribute to the relief of a foreign pressure. A subscription, originating with a sympathetic merchant of New York, had been filled up by many contributors, and a ship named after him, the *George Griswold*, had been freighted with food for the relief of suffering Lancashire. When the *George Griswold* arrived in Liverpool, the Custom House officials had learned from the Government that they had no duties to perform on board; the Liverpool authorities declined to receive dock or town dues; and everybody engaged, down to the dock porters and landing waiters, alike refused to be paid for their services. In this the railway companies joined, carrying the cargo free of cost; while the captain of the ship was made the guest of the Corporation of Liverpool. In New York, stevedores, tug-boats, pilots, shipping-masters, all contributed their services. On his arrival at Liverpool the captain declared he found the steam companies 'vying with each other to tow my ship to port free of charge'.

Thus it was as if in time of war a convoy bringing relief had been thrown into a sorely pressed and starving town. The manifestations of gratitude could not have been more pronounced.

Under such circumstances, Richard Cobden was justified in declaring that the case was totally exceptional. 'The state of affairs', he said, 'has no parallel in all history. It is impossible you could point out to me another case in which, in a limited sphere, such as we have in Lancashire, and in the course of a few months, there has been a cessation of employment at the rate of £7,000,000 sterling per annum in wages. There has been nothing like it in the history of the world for its suddenness, for the impossibility of dealing with it, or managing it in the way of an effective remedy.'

Not until the close of 1862 did the distress show signs of abatement; then, slowly, natural causes brought about a gradual measure of relief. In early December of that year the maximum pressure upon the relief committees was reached. The returns for the last week of December showed 485,434 persons in receipt of aid. The public waited with eager anxiety and with trembling hope for the January return, and when that showed only 451,343 recipients, the rejoicing was mingled with fear lest some mistake should have crept into the figures. The news was thought too good to be true; for there was no visible circumstance to account for the change. Nevertheless, the February report showed a yet further decrease of about 19,000 dependents. The rejoicing now became earnest. It was as if a pestilence was abating, and men shook hands heartily with each other. Instead of the usual empty references to the weather, mutual congratulations were in order to the effect that 'the worst was past'. Though 6,000 persons had been reduced from full to short time since January, the March return showed a further decrease of some 12,000 recipients. April indicated a further and larger decrease of some 58,000; and when June came, the portentous aggregate of those receiving relief had fallen to 256,000. At the end of 1863 it was 180,000. By that time, though still great, the crisis had ceased to be acute.

Things had adjusted themselves. Staking his whole foreign policy upon a single issue, on that issue the Slave-holder had lost. Yet his failure was due to no sudden contingencies lying beyond the ken of human prevision; it was, on the contrary, a complete case of miscalculating over-confidence—unquestioning reliance on a means inadequate to the attainment of the end proposed. Pressure had been mercilessly applied to the full extent possible, every condition contributing to its severity. The Confederacy had meanwhile held its enemy at arm's length during five times the period every Southern authority had fixed upon as ample in which to establish King Cotton's supremacy. Nothing sufficed. The alleged dynasty was fairly and completely dethroned. The bondsman and the growing spirit of nineteenth century self-sacrifice had not been sufficiently taken into account. Conscience had carried it over Cotton; in the jargon of the prize ring Uncle Tom had 'bested' Simon Legree.[2]

It was, however, during the latter half of 1862—those months during which, as has just been seen, the weekly returns of the dependent poor in Lancashire were watched as the bills of mortality in a time of plague—it was during this period when cotton touched thirty pence a pound, that the governmental crisis presented itself. Whether in the American histories of our Civil War, or in the British lives of individuals or general narratives, the story of what then occurred has never received adequate treatment. Passing it over in a way to the last degree superficial, the

[2] See note 2, p. 124.

American authorities have devoted much time and almost unlimited space to an account of indecisive military operations and drawn battles badly fought, utterly ignoring the conflict on the issue of which the struggle at the stage it had then reached virtually depended. The English writers, on the other hand, in a somewhat indifferent spirit, allow a paragraph perhaps for a perfunctory reference to what was in reality for Great Britain's largest textile industry nothing less than a war of emancipation. I propose to-day to fill the historic void, explaining events which in the sequence led to results which are now much in evidence on both sides of the Atlantic; though possibly not exactly in the shape assumed in the outpourings of General Bernhardi's 'Germanic heart'.

In October, 1862, the Queen, widowed only eight months before, had gone over to Germany, and was for a time at Gotha. Earl Russell, the Foreign Secretary, was in attendance upon her. The crisis in American affairs so far as European intervention was concerned now came to a head.

Military operations in America had from the Union point of view then for some time been going steadily from bad to worse. The Confederacy was, on the field of battle, distinctly getting the best of it. So now, referring to the outcome of the so-called 'Pope', or second Bull Run campaign, carried on almost within sight of Washington in August, 1862—those operations in the course of which Lee and 'Stonewall' Jackson so distinguished themselves—Lord Palmerston, then Premier, wrote (September 14th) to Earl Russell at Gotha, suggesting that the time was now come 'for us to consider whether, in such a state of things, England and France might not address the contending parties and recommend an arrangement upon the basis of separation'. This suggestion strongly commended itself to the Foreign Secretary, who immediately replied (September 17th) that he was decidedly of the same mind as the Premier: 'I agree with you that the time is come for offering mediation to the United States Government, with a view to the recognition of the independence of the Confederates. I agree further that, in case of failure, we ought ourselves to recognize the Southern States as an independent State. For the purpose of taking so important a step, I think we must have a meeting of the Cabinet. The 23rd or 20th [October] would suit me for the meeting.' To this very emphatic acquiescence in his views Lord Palmerston, six days later, on the 23rd September, wrote back: 'Your plan of proceedings . . . seems to be excellent. . . . As to the time of making the offer [of mediation], if France and Russia agree—and France, we know, is quite ready and only waiting for our concurrence—events may be taking place which might render it desirable that the offer should be made before the middle of October.'

The course of concurrent events here referred to can be briefly outlined. As I have just said, throughout the months of July and August, 1862, the cause of the Union, east and west, had sustained a series, almost unbroken, of reverses. The Confederacy had not only made good its right to be recognized as a belligerent, but it was a victorious belligerent. Not a single armed Union soldier remained in Virginia outside of the defences of Washington; the war had been carried across the Potomac into Maryland; the national capital itself stood apparently in imminent danger of capture. On the other hand, the Mexican expedition of the French emperor having overrun that country, Napoleon III was urging upon the British Cabinet an aggressive attitude towards the United States; an attitude which would inevitably have proved the first step toward a direct armed intervention. The breaking of the blockade and a renewal of cotton shipments would have followed. Meanwhile the situation in Lancashire seemed fast getting beyond control. If in New York gold stood at a premium of 50, cotton in Liverpool stood at one of 200. The looms, French as well as English, were idle, and a long and sustained wail, a wail of pitiable agony, went up from crowded districts. Whether the fact was then realized in America or not, or has since been recognized by the historian, the hour of crisis was at hand; and the issue was to be settled not on the banks of the Potomac, as generally assumed, but in Downing Street, London.

The Foreign Secretary at this juncture left Gotha, returning to England and his office, where the next two weeks were utilized by him in the preparation of an elaborate, though confidential, Cabinet circular in direct furtherance of the mediation programme. In this circular the question was plainly put to those composing the Cabinet, whether in the light of what had taken place in America and the condition of distress prevailing throughout the manufacturing districts of England and France, it was not the duty of Europe ' to ask both parties, in the most friendly and conciliatory terms, to agree to a suspension of arms' for the purpose of weighing calmly the advantages of peace '—and so forth and so on, in the somewhat unctuous phraseology usual with philanthropic but interested neutrals in times of war-generated stress.

Next to the Premier, Lord Palmerston, and the Foreign Secretary, Earl Russell, Mr. Gladstone, the Chancellor of the Exchequer, was the most influential member of the Cabinet. Consulted as to the proposed programme, he now gave to it his emphatic approval. It entirely coincided with the views he at that time entertained, nor had hesitated to express. The cry of agony coming up from the cotton-spinning districts appealed to his strong humanitarian sympathies; he, like Lord Palmerston, was fully convinced that a re-establishment of the Union was impossible as well as undesirable ; finally, by that subtle process of reasoning always characteristic of him, Mr. Gladstone had persuaded himself that the victory of the slave-owner would ultimately but surely result in the downfall of slavery. He in fact saw, or thought he saw, into the millstone future a little too far. It proved in the result not to be so transparent as he confidently believed it to be.

The concurrence of Mr. Gladstone in the proposed programme rendered assurance doubly sure ; for, as

Lord Granville had a few months before, and in another connexion, written to Lord Canning, 'He [Gladstone], Johnny [Russell], and Pam [Palmerston] are a formidable phalanx when they are united in opposition to the whole Cabinet in foreign matters.' Not only was this so, but in the present case a large majority of the Cabinet were with 'the formidable phalanx'.

Now it was that the wholly unforeseeable, the strangely unexpected, occurred. The meeting of the Cabinet was fixed for the 23rd of October. Mr. Adams, the American Minister to Great Britain, got an inkling of what was on foot. He was sorely disturbed. 'For a fortnight', he wrote, 'my mind has been running so strongly on all this night and day that it seems almost to threaten my life.' For his anxiety, however extreme, he had grounds. The tension was becoming strained to the extent that something, it would seem, must break; and that soon. For, weeks previously, apprehending just such an emergency as was now impending, Mr. Adams had written home asking for specific instructions for his guidance if what he apprehended should speedily occur. Those instructions he had in due time received from Secretary Seward; they were explicit. To make the narrative intelligible, and fully set forth the extreme character of the crisis then impending, these instructions should be read; but, though not long, I have not time here and now to read them in full. Suffice it to say that, carrying the standard entrusted to him high and with a firm hand, the American Secretary then in that hour of darkness, defeat and discouragement bore himself in a way of which his country had cause to be proud. The paper read in part as follows :—

If, contrary to our expectations, the British Government, either alone or in combination with any other Government, should acknowledge the insurgents, while you are remaining without further instructions from this Government concerning that event, you will immediately suspend the exercise of your functions. . . . I have now in behalf of the United States, and by the authority of their chief executive magistrate, performed an important duty. Its possible consequences have been weighed, and its solemnity is therefore felt and freely acknowledged. This duty has brought us to meet and confront the danger of a war with Great Britain and other States allied with the insurgents who are in arms for the overthrow of the American Union. You will perceive that we have approached the contemplation of that crisis with the caution which great reluctance has inspired. But I trust that you will also have perceived that the crisis has not appalled us.

It was with these ringing instructions before him that Mr. Adams, with such fortitude as he could command, now awaited the outcome he was powerless in any material way to affect. The special Cabinet meeting was called for the 23rd of October; to all outward appearance and in all human probability that was the fateful day ; the ordeal must then be faced. The order of exercises was arranged.

The day came ; and passed. Upon it nothing happened. The wholly unexpected had again occurred.

What had taken place? Why was the carefully prepared programme, so far-reaching, so world-momentous, suddenly, quietly, postponed—ostensibly abandoned? It is a curious story; in diplomatic annals scarce any more so. It was, it will be remembered—

for dates in this connexion are all-important—the
23rd of October that had been assigned for the special
Cabinet meeting. Now it so chanced that sixteen
days before, on the 7th of that month, Mr. Gladstone
delivered himself of that famous Newcastle speech,
still remembered, in which he declared that Jefferson
Davis had 'made a nation', and that the independence
of the Confederacy and dissolution of the American
Union were as certain 'as any event yet future and
contingent could be'. That speech, a marvel of indis-
cretion—or, as Mr. Gladstone himself subsequently
expressed it, 'a mistake of incredible grossness'—
though at the moment it caused in the mind of
Mr. Adams a feeling akin to despair, in reality saved
the situation for him and the country he represented.
It was for the American Union a large cash prize
drawn in Fortune's lottery.

Speaking for himself—'playing off his own bat,' as
Lord Palmerston would have expressed it—Mr. Gladstone had foreshadowed a ministerial policy. The
utterance was inspired; in venturing on it Mr. Gladstone unquestionably supposed, as he had good cause
to know, he spoke the minds of both Lord Palmerston
and Lord Russell. The principle of the so-called
'collectivity' of the British Cabinet has been often
discussed, and the rule is well established that minis-
ters are in no wise free to put forward each 'his own
views at large public meetings and elsewhere'. This
Mr. Gladstone had now done. Moreover, it was noto-
rious in ministerial circles that the Prime Minister and
the Chancellor of the Exchequer—Lord Palmerston

and Mr. Gladstone—were not in general harmony.
On the contrary, Lord Palmerston disliked and habitually thwarted Mr. Gladstone ; and Mr. Gladstone
instinctively distrusted Lord Palmerston. A year
before, the two had been ' in violent antagonism' on
financial questions. 'For two months,' Lord Granville,
himself a member of the Cabinet, had written, ' Gladstone had been on half-cock of resignation. . . . Palmerston has tried him hard once or twice by speeches and
Cabinet minutes, and says that the only way to deal
with him is to bully him a little ; and Palmerston',
Granville then went on to say, ' appears to be in the
right.'

A species of Cabinet *modus vivendi* was then arrived
at, and had since been more or less observed ; but the
two men were by nature antagonistic. Built on
wholly different models, they instinctively disliked
each other. Politically, Gladstone, then a man of
fifty-four and in the full maturity of his great powers,
was plainly the coming man ; but Palmerston, so to
speak, though a veteran close on fourscore, held the
fort ; nor did he propose to vacate it in Gladstone's
favour. On the contrary, reading the future not
incorrectly, he had been known to say : ' Gladstone
will soon have it all his own way ; and whenever he
gets my place we shall have strange doings.' It was
a case of armed Cabinet observation.

Under these circumstances, the Chancellor of the
Exchequer had in the autumn of 1862 gone on what
proved to be a sort of triumphal progress through the
northern counties. It amounted to a popular ovation ;

and not unnaturally his colleagues, especially his chief, took cognizance of it. Then came the Newcastle speech. From his long-subsequent published diary entries, it appears that what Mr. Gladstone there said was no hasty, impromptu utterance; it had, on the contrary, been long and well considered. The inference was unavoidable. Distrusting the fixity of the Premier's purpose, the Chancellor of the Exchequer intended to force his hand, thus clinching the thing. In so purposing, Mr. Gladstone had, as a member of the Government, committed an offence against official propriety—again to use his own incomparably forcible characterization, he had been guilty of 'a mistake of incredible grossness.' Apparently it did not take the Premier long to make up his mind that the offender must be disciplined, and that severely; not at all improbably he was glad to avail himself of the opportunity. So he proceeded at once to intimate to Sir George Cornewall Lewis, also a member of the Cabinet and Gladstone's parliamentary rival as the coming man, that if he (Lewis) did not feel disposed to assume this function himself, it must devolve on the head of the Government in person. On the 14th of October, therefore, Sir George Lewis, speaking at Hereford, very pointedly controverted the position taken by his colleague one week before at Newcastle. The hand of the Premier was on the Cabinet lever. The blind goddess had at the critical moment intervened for the preservation of the American Union, and to bring about in ripeness of time the downfall of the Confederacy. On the part of those immediately

concerned as actors it was moreover all undesigned.
Pure chance!

The Cabinet meeting called for the 23rd of October,
the outcome of which had been settled by the concurrence of the Premier, the Foreign Secretary, and
the Chancellor of the Exchequer—Palmerston, Russell and Gladstone—was for the nonce necessarily
postponed; nor was it ever afterwards notified!
Mr. Gladstone had been 'called down'. He having
received a distinct intimation that he was neither the
Ministry nor yet its accredited mouthpiece, explana-
tions on his part were in order. None the less, as
the secret working of the springs and wires which
brought this result about have since been disclosed,
the magnitude and imminence of the danger at that
juncture threatening the cause of the American Union
are revealed. It was a case of touch-and-go.

The hesitation and postponement brought about by
Lord Palmerston in consequence of Mr. Gladstone's
Newcastle speech thus saved the situation. The
veteran Premier at the moment apparently looked
upon it merely as action deferred, probably for a fortnight or a month, more or less. Within that space of
time, as events then indicated, he confidently believed
some definite military result would be reached in
America. Under the vigorous lead of Lee and 'Stonewall' Jackson, the Confederate army might not improbably occupy Washington. And within the period
assigned something did happen!—but not what the
British Premier had anticipated. At just that critical
juncture, and by the merest chance as to time, one of

the great events of the nineteenth century took place
in America. On September 22, while the Prime Minister and the Foreign Secretary were corresponding
with a view to the immediate recognition of the slave-
holding Confederacy, the Emancipation Proclamation
of President Lincoln had been made public. That
African servitude was an issue in the American struggle
could no longer be denied ; the attitude of the national
administration could not be ignored. From that time
the success of the Union cause meant the freedom of
the slave. A conflict of Titans, in the conflict, wholly
regardless of the influence it would have on the
immediate European situation, the quondam Illinois
rail-splitter, by force of circumstances, and quite unconsciously to himself, become transfigured into a
trans-Atlantic Jove, had launched an unmistakable
thunderbolt.

At first, in Europe, and more especially in Great
Britain, the proclamation was not taken seriously ; dazed,
apparently, men seem in no way to have realized its
import. On the contrary, it excited scorn and derision.
I have not time here to give sufficing passages from
the speeches of British public men and the newspaper
editorials of the period ; though they to-day read
curiously. I must confine myself to a few brief
extracts. Mr. Beresford-Hope, for instance, a highly
respectable member of Parliament, energetically characterized the proclamation as 'This slavish type of
weak yet demoniacal spite, the most unparalleled last
card ever played by a reckless gambler'. And a
Mr. Peacock, the member for North Essex, at a great

Conservative demonstration at Colchester towards the close of October, declared that if the proclamation was ' worth anything more than the paper on which it was inscribed, and if the four millions of blacks were really to be emancipated on January 1st [then two months only distant], we should be prepared to witness a carnage so bloody as that even the horrors of the Jacquerie and the massacres of Cawnpore would wax pale in comparison'—and so forth and so on. Furthermore, the proclamation, he declared, was ' one of the most devilish acts of fiendish malignity which the wickedness of man could ever have conceived '. And the London organ of the Confederacy spoke within limits when it declared that while ' every organ of a considerable party pronounced the edict infamous ', a ' similar opinion of it was entertained by every educated and nearly every uneducated Englishman.'

Viewed in the cool, clear perspective of history and through the half-century vista of subsequent events, there is indeed now something distinctly humorous in the simple and honest, but altogether complete self-deception in which the ' educated ' Englishman then nursed himself. What he really objected to, and for the best of reasons from his point of view, was the onward movement towards ' Democracy '—that he felt in the very marrow of his bones ; but he voiced it as follows, the speaker in this case being Mr. G. W. Bentinck, then representing in Parliament West Norfolk. Addressing his constituents at King's Lynn upon American affairs immediately after the appearance of the proclamation, Mr. Bentinck began by

denouncing slavery in general, and American African
servitude in particular. Having set himself perfectly
right by a process of generalization on that point, he
proceeded as follows : 'Why is it that wherever one
goes in all parts of England one always finds—
thoroughly as I believe the institution of slavery is
detested in this country—every man sympathizing
strongly with the Southerners, and wishing them all
success? We do so for this reason . . . Englishmen
love liberty, and the Southerner is fighting, not only
for his life, but for that which is dearer than life, for
liberty ; he is fighting against one of the most grind-
ing, one of the most galling, one of the most irritating
attempts to establish tyrannical government that ever
disgraced the history of the world.' And this was
the view of the Proclamation of Emancipation and
its purport almost universally held at the moment
by the class of which Mr. Bentinck was representative. It was, as the leading London organ of that
class expressed it, an 'atrocious manifesto'. Thus
evoked from the grave to stand a witness in the
strong light of what subsequently occurred, Mr. G. W.
Bentinck is chiefly useful as furnishing additional
evidence of the extreme unwisdom, even in the case
of 'educated gentlemen', of reaching absolute conclusions and expressing fixed opinions upon subjects
in regard to which, where not misinformed, one hap-
pens to be altogether uninformed.

So loud, however, and universal was the denunciation of Lincoln's epoch-marking manifesto—so overwhelming its volume—that, for the moment and

at first, it silenced opposition. The voice of protest
even was dumb. In the entire metropolitan press of
that day one paper only—the *Daily News*—was con-
sistently friendly in tone to the Union side ; and even
the *News* now for a time seemed dazed and daunted.
It referred to the proclamation apologetically, pro-
nouncing it ' feeble and halting ', and in no respect
possessing ' the importance which some persons in
England are disposed to attach to it '. Needless to
say, history has not confirmed this contemporaneous
judgement ; nor at the moment did it commend itself
to John Bright. He, and he first, so far as appears,
rose to the level of the occasion. His attitude was
characteristic ; and, fifty years later, commands that
admiration which at the moment it did not elicit.
Calmly defiant, he faced the storm ; he, almost alone,
seeing beneath the surface and reading correctly what
was passing in the awakened but as yet inarticulate
conscience of England. Wholly uncalled upon to
pronounce himself, he now took immediate advantage of a chance occasion, and uttered the words :
' I applaud the proclamation of the President.' It
was certainly very fine ; fine in its courage, it was
finer yet in its simplicity. In the utterance there was
no bombast, no pose, no attitudinizing or declama-
tion. It went at once to the point. The dignity of
the great drama was sustained.

Curiously enough, and by strange coincidence, the
proclamation and the Newcastle speech of Mr. Gladstone were simultaneous—so much so that they appeared and were commented on in the London journals

of the same week, that closing October 11. Then
came the storm of bitter denunciation of the former;
followed shortly by the still, calm words—'I applaud
the proclamation of the President.'

Though the suffrage had not then been enlarged to
reach the labouring classes, Her Majesty's Governments
of that period were, as is well known, scarcely less
respectful of their wishes on that account; especially
when, as in this instance, a deep-seated moral issue
was plainly involved. So a few weeks later Richard
Cobden wrote to Charles Sumner as follows: 'I now
write to assure you that no unfriendly act on the part
of our Government, no matter which of our aristocratic
parties is in power, towards your cause has yet been
broached. If an attempt were made by the Government in any way to commit us to the South, the
spirit would instantly be aroused which would drive
that Government from power.' Like the stone from
the sling of the son of Jesse, the trans-Atlantic thunderbolt had done its work.

I have thus set forth, I hope in no unnecessary or
uninteresting detail, the influences and course of
events which led to what General Bernhardi has, fifty
years later in the work I have cited, characterized as
the 'unpardonable [British] blunder of not supporting
the Southern States in the American War of Secession'; and also as the supineness of England when
'she refused her assistance to the Southern States and
thus allowed a power to arise in the form of the United
States of North America, which now fifty years later
threatens', according to this authority, 'England's

own position as a World-Power'. I have explained how it all chanced; and, as the secret working of the hidden springs and wires which at the time brought about the final result as now recorded in history have, one by one, been disclosed, the magnitude and intensity of the drama are apparent. It involved at once the discontinuance of human servitude among the civilized, and the continuance of the great English-speaking trans-Atlantic nationality. As respects both, it was a very narrow chance.

The German authority I have quoted asserts that those in charge of Great Britain's interests were then guilty of a blunder, irreparable. To what was their action due?

It was due, I confidently assert, to human causes. Great interests and issues it is true were then involved; great forces were arrayed. England, acting in concert with France, a willing ally in the matter at issue, was master of the situation. Holding indisputably in its hands the mastery of the sea, it had but to say the word and do the deed, and the situation settled itself, the problem was solved. Those responsible for the course of events decided to say the word, and do the deed; yet the word remained unsaid, the deed undone. The course of events then ensued otherwise than it would have been made to ensue. Why was this thus? It was thus, I submit, solely from adventitious causes. A veteran statesman, nearing eighty, was at the critical moment at the head of Her Majesty's Government; himself strongly favouring the success of the insurgent party

in the trans-Atlantic conflict, he fully believed that
the success he desired was in any event assured. In
his conjecture, it was but a question of time and of
the exhaustion of the combatants. Believing that the
hour of crisis had come, he decided on an aggressive
policy, an intervention. Just then an impetuous colleague he did not like undertook to force his hand.
This he resented; and action was accordingly deferred. In his belief it did not matter much; the
American issue was already decided, and decided in
favour of the party he wished to see successful. The
unexpected then occurred. A proclamation ending
human slavery was promulgated; a moral issue presented itself. The parliamentary majority sustaining
the veteran's Government was narrow, and he did not
wish to face a division which could equally well be
avoided. If let alone, the thing was pretty sure satis-
factorily to settle itself; then why provoke an unnecessary home contest? why rouse a sleeping dog?—
the dog in question chancing in this case to be the
British conscience.

Simply, Palmerston misapprehended the situation—
was wrong in his understanding of the facts, and his
anticipation of what was soon to transpire. In other
words, once more the altogether unexpected by him
actually occurred. Hence, and by that mere chance,
the course of subsequent events. None the less, as I
have already said, it was a case of a turn of Fortune's
wheel, with mighty consequences involved.

And such is history! And yet they tell us history
can be reduced to a science. I, on the contrary, hold

that in it chance and the personal equation remain always to be reckoned with. Themistocles at Salamis, close upon twenty-four centuries back, susceptibly influenced by his personality events to-day transpiring in the Balkans; and Harriet Beecher Stowe and Abraham Lincoln in like manner affected for all time what occurred in your Lancashire and Downing Street in 1862. In other words, though the ways of what we are pleased to designate as Providence are mysterious and altogether past finding out, they, all the same, constitute what we call History. If studied in the reverential spirit and with a seeing eye, that History, none the less, has in it, now as then, all the elements of the Greek Tragedy.

Having said thus much, I am loath to run the risk of what may seem to be an anti-climax. Before bringing this lecture to a close, however, one more word. It relates to a great English historical personality— the most notable personality perhaps of the later Victorian period.

The course pursued by Mr. Gladstone, both during the transpiring of the events which have been described and subsequent thereto, was characteristic of the man. Taken altogether also, they were, in my judgement, when not highly creditable to him, not otherwise than creditable. Large by nature, and easily stirred by suffering and wrong, especially when passing directly before his eyes, Mr. Gladstone's course, both in 1862 when Chancellor of the Exchequer and six years later when Prime Minister, though utterly inconsistent, was as respects American affairs, even in its inconsistency, characteristic. During the earlier period, witnessing and sympathizing intensely in the sufferings and distress of his fellow country-people in Lancashire, altogether premature in his conclusions as to the outcome of our trans-Atlantic struggle, Mr. Gladstone had persuaded himself that, from every point of view, a division of the American Union and the establishment of an independent nationality based on African slavery were desirable. Accordingly, he seems at this juncture to have thrown himself into the support of the proposed Palmerston-Russell programme with that fervour of sympathetic conviction peculiarly his. Nor was he chary, much less cautious of utterance, as he afterwards, in the day of his sackcloth and ashes, had good cause to remember and admit. For instance, at the critical period in 1862, he thus wrote in reply to a letter from an American correspondent, in terms unmistakably Gladstonese, setting forth 'the heavy responsibility you [Americans of the North] incur in persevering with this destructive and hopeless war, at the cost of such dangers and evils to yourselves, to say nothing of your adversaries, or of an amount of misery inflicted upon Europe such as no other civil war in the history of man has ever brought upon those beyond its immediate range'. The Chancellor of the Exchequer then went on thus to set forth the wickedness of any further continuance of the efforts towards a re-establishment of the Union: 'The impossibility of success in a war of conquest of itself suffices to make

it unjust. When that impossibility is reasonably
proved, all the horror, all the bloodshed, all the evil
passions, all the dangers to liberty and order with
which such a war abounds, come to lie at the door of
the party which refuses to hold its hand and let its
neighbour be. You know that in the opinion of
Europe that impossibility has [in the present case]
been proved.'

Nevertheless, as we have seen, General Bernhardi
now firmly believes, in view of the existing new-
century later conditions, that in 1862 Mr. Gladstone
was guided by intuitive wisdom in advocating the policy
at one time decided upon but subsequently not pursued.
Urging intervention in our Civil War, he stood ready
to accept every consequence intervention implied.
From his point of view, General Bernhardi possibly
has grounds for his belief; for it is always impossible
to say what would have resulted had something
occurred in the progress of human affairs which it so
chanced did not occur. It is useless, therefore, now
to enter into surmises as to what would, or might,
have happened had the American Union divided in
1862, and the Slave-owning Confederacy established
itself in the face of a growing world-sentiment bound
in the end to make human servitude impossible. We
can only discuss the question with a—*Dis Aliter
Visum!* Mr. Gladstone, however, in reaching his
conclusions in 1862 was, if judged by the actual outcome of events, wrong at every point. That which he
had characterized as ' most improbable, if not altogether
impossible ', actually occurred; and through the tempo-

rary if acute suffering of the population of Lancashire
the world emancipated itself from the dominion of an
industrial staple. That these were both benefits to
the human race no one probably will now deny. They
even justified the great price paid. Mr. Gladstone,
however, as the years passed on, found himself in
a difficult position. It came about in this wise :—All
that Lord Palmerston anticipated happened. When
Palmerston had been five years in his grave, Gladstone
was in his place as Premier ; and in England Gladstone now had it 'all his own way'. But meanwhile
the Franco-Prussian War had brought on the Napoleonic *débâcle* ; the position of Great Britain was
critical ; America was a menace, at once sullen and
portentous. So that Newcastle utterance of Gladstone
in September, 1862, remained to plague him in 1870 ;
it would not away ! True, it was but one of many
similar utterances of that time, and by no means of
the more offensive sort. But, as respects the utterances of public men, no rule obtains, especially with
Democracies. Proverbially ungrateful, when memory
is concerned they are capricious. This was noticeably
the case with us Americans as respects foreign
utterances during our time of tribulation, the wounds
of which were in 1870 still green. The effusions of
the London *Post*, for instance, or the *Saturday Review*,
or *Blackwood* [3], venomous beyond credence, had made no
impression. Idle, as well as flying words, they passed
into early oblivion. Not so in the case of the *Times*.
The editorials of 'The Thunderer' carried a sting,

[3] See Note 3, p. 126.

and the memory of them was stored away to await a
day of reckoning. Later, they furnished at Geneva
a basis for articles of indictment drawn against a whole
people. It was the same with individuals. Displays
of temper, ignorance and vindictiveness on the part
of Mr. Beresford-Hope, or Mr. Peacock, or Mr. W. G.
Bentinck were of no moment; very respectable no
doubt after their kind, they, one and all, were men of
no particular calibre, and what they might say, one
way or the other, mattered not at all. It was not
otherwise with Lord Brougham, then in his garrulous
dotage; nor with the 'Brummagem Brougham,' as
John Bright happily denominated him, the egotistical,
spiteful, cross-grained John Arthur Roebuck; nor,
going higher up, did Lord Wolseley constitute an
exception, harping at one period, unhappily for himself, on 'General' Lee and 'Mr.' Grant; nor again,
higher yet, did it greatly matter that the oracular
sage of Chelsea epigrammatically dismissed it all in
characteristic fashion in the phrase 'a foul chimney
burned out', or delivered himself of an *Ilias Americana
in Nuce*. If men, really eminent, take occasion now
and again to make records for themselves which
they afterwards would fain have comfortably and
kindly forgotten, there is no principle of law, whether
statute or international, violated by their so doing.
Later, no one, not even the unfortunate transgressor
himself, is held to a very grave account. But it was
otherwise in Mr. Gladstone's case. Belonging to
a totally different class, what he publicly said needed
to be well considered, and a Nationality could be

held to account for it.　So it in due time followed that among all the utterances of English journalists and British public men in that period of voluble utterance, that Newcastle speech of his, then Chancellor of the Exchequer but now Premier, was retained most freshly in American memory.[4]　An envenomed barb, it penetrated deep and rankled sorely.　By it he had made himself, if not actually odious, at least suspect in the American mind ; and the 'insensate' and 'degenerate' people of the *Times* had now become that same journal's 'mighty Republic beyond the sea.'　There is equally little question that America subsequently to 1865 held itself ready when occasion offered, and it was sure to offer, to apply to Great Britain that rule of action which in its hour of stress had been applied to it.　So, when Great Britain stood face to face with foreign complications directly following the outbreak of the Franco-German War, had things gone a step further, resulting in declared hostilities, the ocean might readily have been covered with commerce-destroyers—*Alabamas* emerging from American ports.

An ordinary public man, especially perhaps an ordinary English public man, would, under these circumstances, have been naturally inclined to stand by his record ; as he had put himself in the wrong, he would have stayed in the wrong, challenging consequences.　Mr. Gladstone was by nature and training quite above this small consistency so dear to little minds.　He consequently met the contingency, when it presented itself during his first period of responsibility in a large way ; and, absolutely reversing his earlier course and utterances, recognizing as such his 'mistake of incredible grossness', he accomplished one of the largest results, if not on the whole the largest and most valuable result, of his public life, at once so memorable and in results so fruitful. He restored, in the only way in which it could be restored, mutual goodwill and friendly feeling between the two great English-speaking communities. I refer, of course, to the Treaty of Washington, negotiated in 1870, and the Geneva arbitration, which in pursuance of its provisions sat in 1872. Up to the time of the negotiation of the Treaty of Washington it is not too much to say that a feeling of bitter animosity towards Great Britain prevailed in both the loyal portion of the American Union and in that which had once been the Confederacy. Both sides, and especially that element in each of the two sides which represented the military life of the War of Secession, looked forward to a severe retribution as sure, in the not remote future, to fall to the lot of Great Britain. This feeling Mr. Gladstone met and overcame. Also, he did so, I again say, in a very large way, the only way possible. And, so carrying himself, he re-established friendly feeling on the opposite sides of the Atlantic. On the basis then reached this feeling of kindly kinship has now held for nearly half a century, and we have sufficient reason to hope that it will continue to hold.

This last is, however, a larger topic, and, as respects it, I shall in my present course confine myself to this passing reference.

Note 1, Page 91.

The following extracts from Watts's *Facts of the Cotton Famine* sufficiently illustrate the fluctuations in the price of cotton and in the fortunes of those trading in it—fluctuations almost continuous throughout this period :—

In September [1863] discounts again advanced to eight or nine per cent; middling Orleans was at thirty-one pence, and shirtings were thirty-three pence per pound; and again employment decreased. But another and a more powerful cause than the price of discounts was now at work. For three and a half years had the terrible American struggle gone on with the usual varying fortunes of war, and trade was gradually accommodating itself to war prices, when a rumour crossed the Atlantic that men were meeting at Niagara Falls to try to arrange the terms of peace. Straightway men, instead of shaking hands and throwing up their hats in thankfulness that the mutual slaughter of their American brethren was at an end, looked into each other's faces with blank despair, as if peace, instead of war, was the greatest curse upon earth. Nor was it without reason that this fear and terror was felt and expressed. Middling Orleans cotton fell from thirty-one pence to twenty-three pence half-penny, and shirtings from thirty-three pence to twenty-four pence per pound; and men who held largely of cotton, twist or cloth, found their fortunes vanished in a night at the breath of this rumour. All trade arrangements were again in chaos. . . .

. . . In the beginning of the year 1865 the Bombay correspondent of *The Times* wrote to the following effect: Up to 1860 the sum paid by Europe for the whole cotton export of India was not above seven millions sterling annually. In 1860–1 the import of bullion into Bombay alone was six and one-third millions sterling, chiefly in payment for cotton. But in the three following years, Europe paid to India nearly forty millions sterling per annum, one half of which was in bullion. In Calcutta the trade is almost entirely in the hands of Europeans, the Bengalese playing but a subordinate part. But in Bombay the trade is largely in the hands of the caste-less native Parsees ; and many of them, and a smaller number of Scotchmen, who a few years ago were petty brokers, are now millionaires. A Hindoo, named Premchund Roychund, lately a subordinate clerk in an English house on £30 a year, has by daring speculation amassed two millions sterling. Rustonjee, the second son of the late Sir Jamsetjee Jejeebhoy, who inherited but a moderate fortune, has become the millionaire of Bombay, his capital being reckoned at two and a half millions sterling. Twenty such cases could be mentioned. . . .

. . . Mr. Henry Ashworth, speaking at the annual meeting of the Manchester Chamber of Commerce, 30th January, 1865, said : 'The quantity of cotton consumed in 1860 was valued at £34,000,000. Last year (1864), for a quantity probably not exceeding one-half what we received in 1860, we had to pay, in round numbers, £80,000,000. In 1860 our consumption was one billion eighty-three million pounds. In 1864 it was five hundred and sixty-one million pounds, or about fifty-one per cent. of the former year. But the inferiority of the material required much more labour ; hence the fifty-one per cent. of cotton consumed required from sixty to seventy per cent. of the hands to work it up. In 1860 American cotton furnished five days' labour out of six in every week ; in 1864 it did not furnish enough for half a day per week. In 1860 we paid for Indian cotton £3,500,000, and in 1864 nearly £40,000,000. The quantity had increased two and a half times (from two hundred and fourteen million pounds to five hundred and thirteen million pounds), and the price had increased ten or eleven times.'

The highest point reached by cotton in America was on August 23, 1864, when, in the greatly depre-ciated paper currency then in use, middling upland sold for $1.89 per pound on the New York market, and for $1.95 in Boston.   Eight months later the price fell to 35 cents.

NOTE 2, PAGE 97.

The view in these lectures advanced as to the origin of the American Civil War, the theories, economical and otherwise, upon which those constituting the Confederacy challenged the trial of strength, and the influence of *Uncle Tom's Cabin* upon public opinion, were at the time appreciated in Europe and distinctly stated.   For example, a French writer, Eugene Pelletan, thus expressed himself upon these points, somewhat theatrically addressing his paper to the potentate then, as in these lectures, commonly designated as ' King Cotton ' : —

But one day an honest man named John Brown tried to discover whether there were any pulsation left beneath the negro's cotton shirt.   This was an error, I admit.   You seized the noble champion of humanity, you tried him, and you hung him.   Bravo, sir, I recognize you by this act of clemency, for you could have burnt him alive at the stake ! But when he was executed a great shudder swept through the North of America.   Thenceforth the sacred cause of Abolitionism was invested with the halo of martyrdom.

It had already sounded its tocsin, in the shape of a paltry little book written by a woman ; and it was less than a book, it was a novel.   You smiled compassionately at it, did you not ?   Your children may cry over it for a long while. America read Mrs. Stowe's elegy and bewailed her state ; and the presidency of Abraham Lincoln sprang from the presidency of Uncle Tom.

I breathe again.   I have rid me of a nightmare, for the time for justice had arrived : right is not a lie.   Scarcely had the South learned the election of Lincoln before with their impious hand, already polluted with the blood of the slave, they dared to strike their mother, to strangle the Constitution, throwing to the winds the common glory of their common country, telling the Union their intention to walk thenceforward independently with the negro trampled beneath their feet.

You, sire, and you alone, without provocation or excuse, have broken the compact which you signed and swore to keep. In your rebellious folly you said to yourself, ' What have I to fear from the North, from the lovers of peace and dollars ? Will they dare to raise an army for the abstract satisfaction of unity ? And supposing that they dare, I need only hold fast to my bales of cotton. At one blow I can cause a famine in all the markets of Europe, and array all the spindles and looms of Manchester and Mulhouse against these fanatical Yankees and their Constitution. Then England and France must of necessity—either jointly or separately— intervene in favour of slavery in order to save their cotton.

' And if they hesitate, if they shrink from armed mediation, what will they do with their disbanded hosts of cotton-spinners ? Will they be allowed to wander at random, pale and ragged, like the spectres of famine, about the extinguished furnaces and silent factories, until at last, tired of suffering, they make one desperate effort and throw themselves upon the bayonets of their countrymen ? Certainly not ; France as well as England must prefer to open the Southern markets at any cost, even by force of shot and shell.'

This is the impious calculation you made when you rebelled against the Constitution. You condemned the poorer classes of Europe to want for work, in other words, to a slow death, so as to preserve slavery in all its purity ; after adding another crime to your list, you hauled down the federal flag waving over Fort Sumter.

An Address to King Cotton. By Eugene Pelletan. Loyal Pub. Socy., No. 12, 1863.

NOTE 3, PAGE 118.

Extracts from an editorial paper in *Blackwood's Edinburgh Magazine* for November, 1863, Vol. XCIV:—

If we were required to specify the most prominent and characteristic feature exhibited in common by the Government, press, and people of Federal America, we should say it was shameless impudence—impudence which tramples on consistency and derides confutation. It has appeared in every pretence they have put forward for the justification of the war. Something more than chance seems to have guided them in their unerring choice of arguments that never deviate into plausibility, and assertions that never stumble on the truth. . . . They profess that what has more than anything raised the indignation of their guileless and virtuous citizens is the treachery with which secession was accomplished—as if the most characteristic and most applauded feature in Federal diplomacy had not always been triumphant chicanery. Ignorant alike of the foundation and the value of their liberty, and ready to sacrifice at the shrine of any detestable and ridiculous idol that chances to govern the hour, they persist in proclaiming their effort to enslave the South as a ' battle for freedom.' . . . Manifestly, the element visible in all this is impudence, pure and simple. There is no plausibility in these utterances—no consistency, no faith on the part of the utterers. The matter being what we have said, there is certainly nothing in the manner which should render them more acceptable. Whether they proceed from clergymen, or senators, or stump-orators, from press or people, they are equally distinguished by repulsive coarseness, vulgarity, and inconsequence. . . . If [the States composing the Confederacy] ever had a talent for bombast and boasting, they appeared to have lost that useful faculty when they seceded from the Union, leaving the North to enjoy the double share. All their appeals have been made rather by acts and demeanour than words. Dignity in misfortune, modesty and moderation in success ; conduct in council, bravery in the field ; the exhibition, in a struggle for that independence which free nations have always professed most to value, of a constancy and heroism almost unequalled ; the endurance of uncommon calamities with cheerfulness, and the absence of vindictiveness under the most hideous provocation ;—such are the demands the South makes on us—and the results are not encouraging to the heroic virtues. . . . If the North had little claim on our forbearance at the outset of the quarrel, it has far less now. It is generally agreed in England that this power which we so scrupulously refrain from embarrassing is persisting in a hopeless war from the basest motives, and conducting it in a way that casts mankind back two centuries towards barbarism. We say, then, that if, by joining France in intervention, we should raise the blockade, relieve our starving population, and break up the political system which is a standing menace to us through the weak point of Canada, we should be not only acting in consonance with right, but fulfilling an obvious duty to ourselves.

The following is from the issue for January, 1863 :—

We will not follow Mr. Cobden's hypothetical view of what would be done if in America there were now 'men of the grasp of mind of a Franklin, a Jefferson, an Adams, or a Washington'. No such men exist nowadays. Those men were all of them trained as British subjects. We have now before us the result of a democratic training, and it speaks for itself. Our business is to deal not with the departed, but the present rulers of that distracted country.

So in the May number of the same magazine the United States is thus referred to : 'the system, be it remembered, whose inevitable results have been to make a Lincoln the chief magistrate, and a Seward the chief minister—a system which has for years been the most corrupt ever known, and the inability of which to produce any kind of political merit is one of the wonders of the world.'

Note 4, Page 120.

Writing thirty-four years later, Mr. Gladstone thus, again characteristically, referred to this experience, of which, in the language of Lord Morley, his biographer, 'he was destined never to hear the last':—

I have yet to record, he writes (July, 1896), in the fragment already more than once mentioned, an undoubted error, the most singular and palpable, I may add the least excusable of them all, especially since it was committed so late as in the year 1862, when I had outlived half a century. In the autumn of that year, and in a speech delivered after a public dinner at Newcastle-upon-Tyne, I declared in the heat of the American struggle that Jefferson Davis had made a nation; that is to say, that the division of the American Republic by the establishment of a Southern or Secession State was an accomplished fact. Strange to say, this declaration, most unwarrantable to be made by a Minister of the Crown with no authority other than his own, was not due to any feeling of partisanship for the South or hostility to the North. . . . Not only was this a misjudgement of the case, but, even if it had been otherwise, I was not the person to make the declaration. I really, though most strangely, believed that it was an act of friendliness to all America to recognize that the struggle was virtually at an end. I was not one of those who on the ground of British interests desired a division of the American Union. My view was distinctly opposite. I thought that while the Union continued it never could exercise any dangerous pressure upon Canada to estrange it from the empire—our honour, as I thought, rather than our interest forbidding its surrender. But were the Union split, the North, no longer checked by the jealousies of slave-power, would seek a partial compensation for its loss in annexing, or trying to annex, British North America. Lord Palmerston desired the severance as a diminution of a dangerous power, but prudently held his tongue.

That my opinion was founded upon a false estimate of the facts was the very least part of my fault. I did not perceive the gross impropriety of such an utterance from a Cabinet Minister of a power allied in blood and language, and bound to loyal neutrality. . . . My offence was indeed only a mistake, but one of incredible grossness, and with such consequences of offence and alarm attached to it that my failing to perceive them justly exposed me to very severe blame. It illustrates vividly that incapacity which my mind so long retained, and perhaps still exhibits, an incapacity of viewing subjects all round, in their extraneous as well as in their internal properties, and thereby of knowing when to be silent and when to speak.—Morley, *Life of Gladstone*, Vol. II, pp. 81–82.

IV

A GREAT HISTORIC CHARACTER

AND

VAE VICTIS

IV

A GREAT HISTORIC CHARACTER

AND

VAE VICTIS

In the course of his memorable, and still remembered, speech on American taxation, delivered in the House of Commons in 1774, Edmund Burke made use of this expression, 'Great men are the guideposts and landmarks in the State.' In no way original or profound, the figure of speech is none the less peculiar to him who then made use of it—it bears Burke's unmistakable mint-mark. But the question next naturally arises as to those fairly entitled to be classed as 'great men'. Posterity has a way in such cases of calling for credentials : which, on inspection, are not infrequently pronounced defective and insufficient. In the case, for instance, of those by name passed on by Burke in the speech referred to—George Grenville, Charles Townshend and the rest—not one is to-day recalled as 'great'. Gone from memory, they abide only as names attached to shades lurking amid the urns and sepulchres of the parliamentary graveyard. Among the wellnigh innumerable public characters of that somewhat commonplace period Burke himself was 'great'; so also was Chatham. The rest, conspicuous enough in their day, when not completely forgotten are at best but vaguely recalled.

American history now covers four centuries. Reaching back to the first Tudor, four centuries constitute a very respectable antiquity. During those centuries, how many world celebrities—those entitled to be classed among the really 'great'—has America produced? Three might, I suppose, be very generally accepted—the credentials of Washington, Franklin, and Lincoln bear closest scrutiny. All others would, I fancy, be challenged. Of the three I have named enough has, however, been said. They are thrice-told tales; so to-day it is my purpose to examine another set of credentials, seeking to learn why the bearer of them should not also be classified among the 'great', completing an American quartette, so to speak—our constellation.

Among those inhabiting the region once calling itself the Confederate States of America there is no question that Robert Edward Lee is the ideal, the memory most cherished. In him, more than in any other one man, is personified what throughout a large and now wholly loyal section is still referred to as 'The Lost Cause'.

In connexion with it, he stands much as Hannibal stands in his connexion with another no less 'lost cause' twenty-one centuries before. In a recent careful study of Lee, by one who has given to his subject much thought and thorough inquiry, I find it asserted that I individually have by my utterances 'surely done more than any one else to help Lee on to the national glory which is his due.' Whether this be so or not, to-day, and Oxford here is a sufficiently appropriate arena for the purpose, I propose to essay a more ambitious flight. The authority I have just quoted spoke of 'national glory'. I ambition a larger theme, world fame. It so chances, however, that Lee suggests himself just now in a way most opportune with these lectures of mine; for he illustrates, as no other does or could, certain of the historical features connected with our American development which I have endeavoured to emphasize and explain. And, first, State Sovereignty.

I do not propose here and now to enter into any eulogium of General Lee, to recount the incidents of his career, or to estimate the place finally to be assigned him among great military commanders. This has been sufficiently done by others far better qualified than I for the task. I shall also assume on the part of my audience a certain general acquaintance with essential historic facts. Coming then directly to the matter in hand, my own observation tells me that the charge still most commonly made against Lee in that section of my own country to which I belong and with which I sympathize is that, in plain language, he was false to his flag. Educated at the national military academy, subsequently an officer of the United States Army, he abjured his allegiance and bore arms against the Government he had sworn to uphold. In other words, he was a military traitor. I state the charge in the tersest language possible; and the facts are as stated! Having done so, and, for the purpose of the present occasion, admitting the facts, I add as the result of mature reflection, that under exactly similar conditions I would myself have done as Lee did. In fact, I do not see how, placed as he was placed, any other course was, humanly speaking, open to him.

And now, fairly entered on the first phase of my theme, I must hurry on; for I have much ground to cover, and scant time in which to cover it. I must be concise, but must not fail to be explicit. And first as to the right or wrong of secession, this theoretically.

State Sovereignty, so called, as a feature in the development of American nationality, I discussed, sufficiently I hope, in the initial lecture of the present course. In any event, I do not propose to repeat what I then said, thus twice going over the same ground.

Coming directly to the point, my contention, it will be remembered, was that every man in the eleven States seceding from the Union had in 1861, whether he would or no, to decide for himself whether to adhere to his State or to the Nation; and finally I asserted that, whichever way he decided, if only he decided honestly, putting self-interest behind him, he decided right.

This to foreign ears sounds, I know, like a contradiction in terms; none the less it was indisputably so. It was a question of sovereignty, and consequent allegiance—State or National; and from a decision of that question there was in a seceded State escape for no man.

Starting from this as a premise, I pass on to Lee's individual case. Lee was not a Secessionist; and he did hold a commission in the United States Army. A man of fifty-four, he had in March, 1861, become colonel of the 1st Cavalry. Though a Virginian, he had, with intuitive common sense, at the outset struck the nail squarely on the head, when amid the Babel of discordant voices heralding the outbreak of active hostilities he wrote to his son, ' It is idle to talk of secession '; the national government, as it had then got to be, ' can only be dissolved by revolution.' This puts the case in a nutshell ; and the human, the individual element now entered as a dominant factor, indeed the controlling factor, in its solution.

People had to elect ; the *modus vivendi* was at an end. Was the State sovereign; or was the Nation sovereign? And, with a shock of genuine surprise that any doubt should exist on that head, eleven States arrayed themselves on the side of the sovereignty of the State, and claimed the unquestioning allegiance of their citizens ; and I think it not unsafe to assert that nowhere did the original spirit of State Sovereignty and allegiance to the State then survive in greater intensity and more unquestioning form than in Virginia—the ' Old Dominion '—the mother of States and of Presidents. And here I approach a sociological factor in the problem, more subtle, and also more potent, than any legal consideration. It has no standing in court ; but the historian may not ignore it: while, with the biographer of Lee, it is crucial. Upon it judgement hinges. I have not time to consider how or why such a result came about, but of the fact there can, I hold, be no question —State pride, a sense of individuality, has immemorially entered more largely and more intensely into Virginia and Virginians than into any other section or

community of the United States.   Only in South Carolina and among Carolinians, on the trans-Atlantic continent, was a somewhat similar sense of locality and
obligation of descent to be found.   There was in it a
flavour of the Hidalgo, or of the pride which the Mac-
Gregors and Campbells took in their clan and country.
In other words, the Virginian and Carolinian had in
the middle of the last century not, to any appreci-
able extent, undergone nationalization.

But this, it will be replied, though true of the
ordinary man and citizen, should not have been true
of the graduate of the military academy—the officer
of the Army of the United States.   Winfield Scott and
George H. Thomas—both Virginians, both in 1861
holding commissions in the national army, and the
last named not only a graduate of the military
academy in the same class with Lee, but in 1861
an officer in the same regiment—Lieutenant-General
Winfield Scott and Major, afterwards Major-General
George H. Thomas, did not so construe their allegiance ; when the issue was presented, they remained
true to their flag and to their oaths.   Robert E. Lee,
false to his oath and flag, was a renegade !   And, as
a rule, renegades are not included among the truly
great of the world.   The answer is brief and to the
point : the conditions in the several cases cited were
not the same—neither Scott nor Thomas was Lee.
It was our Boston Dr. Holmes, the freshly remembered Autocrat of the Breakfast Table, who long ago
declared that the child's education begins about one
hundred and fifty years before it is born ; and it is

quite impossible to separate any man—least of all, perhaps, a full-blooded Virginian—from his pre-natal conditions and living environment. From them he drew his being; in them he exists. Robert E. Lee was the embodiment of those conditions, the creature of that environment—a Virginian of Virginians. His father was 'Light-Horse Harry' Lee, a devoted follower of Washington; but in January, 1792, 'Light-Horse Harry' wrote to Mr. Madison, ' No consideration on earth could induce me to act a part, however gratifying to me, which could be construed into disregard of, or faithlessness to, this Commonwealth'; and later, when in 1798 those Virginia and Kentucky resolutions to which I have in these lectures already referred as first embodying the principle of secession—when, I say, these fateful resolutions were in 1798 under discussion in the legislature of Virginia, so-called, 'Light-Horse Harry' exclaimed in words, so far as his son was concerned, ominously prophetic, 'Virginia is my country; her will I obey, however lamentable the fate to which it may subject me.' Born in this environment, nurtured in these traditions, to ask Lee to raise his hand against Virginia was like asking Montrose or the MacCallum More to lead a force designed for the subjection of the Highlands and the destruction of the clans. Where such a stern election is forced upon a man as then confronted Lee, the single thing the fair-minded investigator has to take into account is the loyalty, the single-mindedness of the election. Was it devoid of selfishness? Was it free from any baser and more worldly motive? Was ambition, pride, jealousy, revenge, or self-interest eliminated? To these questions there can, in the case of Lee, be but one answer.

One April night in 1861 he paced the floor at Arlington, the lights of Washington gleaming in the distance across the broad Potomac, and then, after long and trying mental wrestling, he threw in his fate with Virginia. In doing so he knowingly sacrificed everything which man prizes most, his dearly beloved home, his means of support, his professional standing, his associates, a brilliant future assured him. Born a slaveholder in a race of slaveholders, he was himself no defender, much less an advocate of slavery; on the contrary, in his place he did not hesitate to pronounce it 'a moral and political evil'. Later, he manumitted his bondsmen. He did not believe in secession; as a right reserved under the Constitution he pronounced it 'idle talk': but, as a Virginian, he also added, 'if the Government is disrupted, I shall return to my native State and share the miseries of my people, and save in defence will draw my sword on none.' Next to his high sense of allegiance to Virginia was Lee's pride in his profession. He was a soldier; as such rank, and the possibility of high command and great achievement, were very dear to him. His choice put rank and command behind him. He quietly and silently made the greatest sacrifice a soldier can be asked to make. With war plainly impending, the foremost place in the army of which he was an officer was now tendered him; his answer was to lay down the commission he already held.

Virginia had been drawn into the struggle; and, though he recognized no necessity for the state of affairs, 'in my own person,' he wrote, 'I had to meet the question whether I should take part against my native State; I have not been able to make up my mind to raise my hand against my relatives, my children, my home.' It may have been treason to take this position; the man who took it, uttering these words and sacrificing as he sacrificed, may have been technically a renegade to his flag—if you please, false to his allegiance: but he stands awaiting sentence at the bar of history in very respectable company—for instance, in that of William of Orange, known as The Silent. Those composing it were, one and all, in the sense referred to, false to their oaths—forsworn.

In Virginia, Lee was MacGregor; and, where Mac-Gregor sits, there is the head of the table.

Into Lee's subsequent career, I can here only very briefly enter; nor shall I undertake to compare him with other great military characters, whether contemporaneous or of all time. Not only has the topic been discussed by others [1], not always to my mind with either judgement or good taste, but the space limitation here again confronts me. I must press on. Suffice it for me, as one of those then opposed in arms to Lee,

[1] Lord Acton pronounced Lee 'the greatest general the world has ever seen, with the possible exception of Napoleon'. Writing sixteen years after the occurrence, he used the expression that he rejoiced in a certain event 'more than I have been able to feel at any public event ever since I broke my heart over the surrender of Lee'.

in however subordinate a capacity, to admit at once
that, as a leader, he conducted operations on the highest plane.   Whether acting on the defensive upon the
soil of his native State, or leading his army into the
enemy's country, he was humane, self-restrained, and
strictly observant of the most advanced rules of civilized warfare.   He respected the non-combatant; nor
did he ever permit the wanton destruction of private
property.

But though avoiding any critical discussion, I will
generally say that, to my mind and in my judgement,
Lee's first was his most brilliant campaign; indeed
I do not see why it will not bear comparison with the
most brilliant of historic campaigns under the greatest
commanders.   It was in July, 1862.   When at that
time suddenly placed in command of a large army,
face to face with an enemy of greatly superior force,
Lee was a man of fifty-five; almost exactly the age
of Marlborough when he assumed his first large command in the Blenheim campaign.   Never before at the
head of any considerable force, Lee was then acting
as military adviser of Jefferson Davis, President of the
Confederacy.   In those days the present elaborate
general staff organizations were undreamed of, the
traditions and organizations of the Napoleonic period
and the Crimea still prevailing.   Himself a graduate
of the national military academy, and not without
active military experience, President Davis divined
Lee's capacity, and looked to him largely for advice,
and the confirmation, or otherwise, of his own conclusions.   Just at this juncture General Joseph E.

Johnston, in command of the Confederate forces defending Richmond, was incapacitated by injuries received in battle, and Davis at once designated Lee to succeed him.

When, in those fierce contesting days of 1862, Lee thus, while the battle was in progress, assumed command, the armies of the Union—of the North as it was called—were pressing hard on the Confederate capital. Though they did not realize the fact, and immensely exaggerated the number and equipment of those opposed to them, they were to their enemy at least as two or three to one : but, badly commanded, they were operating as at least four separate organizations, advancing by different lines on a common objective, while yet carefully covering Washington, whence they received directions. As a military situation, it was open to criticism at every point. With what then ensued, you here in England are not unacquainted. Colonel Henderson's *Life of 'Stonewall' Jackson* is a text-book at Sandhurst; and Robert E. Lee's name is almost a household word in Great Britain. Suffice it to say that, knowing the country well and superbly supported by his lieutenants and the unsurpassed fighting material of which his army was composed, throwing his force first in one direction and then in another, always outnumbering his antagonists at the immediate critical point, in less than sixty days from his taking command Lee had completely cleared Virginia of its enemies, and was himself carrying the war into the enemy's country. Washington, not Richmond, was in danger of capture.

It was a great military achievement.   Taking all the circumstances of the case into consideration, I know of none more brilliant; though, of course, many have been both more considerable, and some, perhaps, more dramatic.   In effective completeness, however, it will compare with any; for it was perfect in its kind.   Lee had everything except mere numbers in his favour; and he availed himself boldly and skilfully of his advantages.   Napoleon did no more in Italy in 1796; or Wellington in the Peninsula in 1813.

Of Lee's two succeeding campaigns, that of Fredericksburg in the closing weeks of 1862, and that of Chancellorsville in the April following, I have not time to speak; nor do I wish to talk, or even think, of them. I participated, of course on the Union side, in both; and their memory is still very bitter to me.   It recalls hardship, failure, and the useless loss of precious lives.   The Fredericksburg folly should never have been entered upon; the campaign of Chancellorsville should have been for us a brilliant success.   In both cases the Union army was wretchedly handled; and Lee proved equal to the occasion.   The Army of the Potomac sustained two severe repulses, involving terrible loss of both life and prestige.

But why enlarge?   Comparisons are always invidious, and I feel no disposition here to institute them : but some things are too obvious to admit of denial. Almost every military aphorism is as a matter of course attributed to Napoleon; and so Napoleon is alleged first to have remarked that 'In war men are

nothing, a man is everything'.[1] And, as formerly
a soldier of the Army of the Potomac, I now stand
appalled at the risk I unconsciously ran anterior to
July, 1863, when confronting the Army of Northern
Virginia, commanded as it then was and as we were.
The situation was in fact as bad with us in the Army
of the Potomac as it was with the Confederates in
the south-west. There the unfortunate Pemberton
simply was not in the same class as Grant and Sherman, to whom he found himself opposed. Results
followed accordingly. Vicksburg fell; the Mississippi
flowed free to the sea; the Confederacy was cut in
twain. So in Virginia, Lee, Jackson and Longstreet
constituted together a most exceptional combination.
They outclassed McClellan and Burnside, Pope and
Hooker, in quick succession our commanders; outclassed them sometimes terribly, sometimes ludi-
crously, always hopelessly : and again results followed
accordingly. That we were not utterly destroyed
affords a marked and, for us, most creditable exception
to the general truth of Napoleon's aphorism.

Though fifty years have since elapsed, well do I
remember the feeling of relief, almost of exultation,
I individually felt when one April day the rumour
spread through our crestfallen camp at Acquia Creek,
opposite Fredericksburg, that 'Stonewall' Jackson
was dead—a victim of wounds received in the battle
which had just been fought; and, by us, lost. After
all it had been a victory; for Jackson's 'foot-cavalry'

[1] 'A la guerre les hommes ne sont rien, c'est un homme qui
est tout.'

T

would not again come yelling and volleying around our uncovered flank.

The Gettysburg campaign followed close on the heels of that of Chancellorsville ; it opened before Jackson had been a month in his grave. Gettysburg marked the turning-point in the military fate of the Confederacy. From that day (July 4, 1863) its star began to descend, to sink for ever below the horizon just twenty-one months later (April 9, 1865). That Gettysburg campaign is burned very deep into my memory as an active participant therein, and the views I entertain of it are not in all respects those generally held ; so I cannot dismiss it with mention only.

Studied in the light of results, Lee's action in that campaign has been criticized : his crucial attack on Gettysburg's third day has been pronounced a murderous persistence in a misconception ; and, among Confederate writers especially, the effort has been to relieve him of responsibility for final miscarriage, transferring it to his lieutenants. As a result reached from participation in those events and subsequent study of them, briefly let me say I concur in none of these conclusions. Taking the necessary chances incident to all warfare on a large scale into consideration, the Gettysburg campaign was on the Confederate part in my opinion timely, admirably designed, energetically executed, and brought to a close with consummate military skill. A well-considered offensive thrust of the most deadly character, intelligently aimed at the opponent's heart, its failure was of the narrowest; and the disaster to the defeated side which that failure might readily have involved was no less skilfully than successfully averted.

I cannot here and now enter into details. But I hold that credit, and the consequent measure of applause, in the outcome of that campaign belong to Lee's opponent and not to him. All the chances were in Lee's favour, and he should have won a great victory; while Meade should have sustained a decisive defeat. As it was, Meade triumphantly held his ground; Lee suffered a terrible repulse. His deadly thrust was foiled; his campaign was a failure.

But, so far as Lee's general plan of operations, and the movements which culminated in the battle of Gettysburg, were concerned, be it always and ever remembered, a leader must, in war, take some chances, and mistakes will occur; but the mistakes are rarely, if ever, all on one side. They tend to counterbalance each other; and, commanders and commanded being at all equal, not unseldom it is the balance of misconceptions, shortcomings, miscarriages, and the generally unforeseen, and indeed unforeseeable, which tips the scale to victory or defeat.

In the Gettysburg campaign—and I actually participated in it from its opening to its close—every personal recollection of what then occurred, as well as my study of it since, lead me to believe that in its earlier stages the preponderance of the accidental was distinctly in Lee's favour. On any fair weighing of chances, he should have won a decisive victory; as matter of actual outcome, he and his army ought to have been destroyed. As usual, on that theatre of war at that time, neither result came about.

First, as to the chapter of accidents—the misconceptions, miscarriages and shortcomings. If, as has been alleged, an essential portion of Lee's force was at one time out of reach and touch, and if, at the critical moment, a lieutenant was not promptly in place at a given hour, on the Union side an unforeseen change of supreme command went into effect when battle was already joined, and the newly appointed commander had no organized staff; his army was not concentrated; his strongest corps was over thirty miles from the point of conflict; and the two corps immediately engaged should have been destroyed in detail before reinforcements could have reached them. In addition to all this—superadded thereto—the most skilful general and perhaps the fiercest fighter on the Union side was killed at the outset. Later, and at a most critical moment, Meade's line of battle was almost fatally disordered by the misconception of a corps commander. The chapter of accidents thus reads all in Lee's favour. But, while Lee on any fair weighing of chances stands in my judgement more than justified both in his conception of the campaign and in every material strategic move made in it, he none the less fundamentally misconceived the situation, with consequences which should have been fatal both to him and to his command. Frederick did the same at Kunersdorf; Napoleon at Waterloo. In the first place, Lee had at that time supreme confidence in his command; and he had sufficient ground therefor. As he himself then wrote,

'There never were such men in any army before. They will go anywhere and do anything, if properly led.' And, for myself, I do not think the estimate thus expressed was exaggerated; speaking deliberately, having faced some portions of the Army of Northern Virginia at the time, and having reflected much on the occurrences of that momentous period, I do not believe that any more formidable or better organized and animated force was ever set in motion than that which Lee led across the Potomac in the early summer of 1863. It was essentially an army of fighters—men who, individually or in the mass, could be depended on for any feat of arms in the power of mere mortals to accomplish. They would blanch at no danger. This Lee from experience knew. He had tested them; they had implicit confidence in him. He also thought he understood his opponent; for he had faced him recently at Chancellorsville. Meade had not yet succeeded Hooker.

The disasters which had befallen the Confederates in the south-west in the spring and early summer of 1863 had to find compensation in the east. The exigencies of warfare necessitated it. Some risk must be incurred. So Lee determined to assume the offensive, to carry the war into the enemy's country. Then came the rapid, aggressive move; and the long, desperately contested struggle of Gettysburg, culminating in that historic charge of Pickett's Virginia division. Paradoxical as it may sound in view of the result, that charge—what those men did—justified Lee. True, those who made the charge did not accomplish the impossible ; but towards it they did all that mortal men could do.   But it is urged that Lee should have recognized the impossible when face to face with it, and not have directed brave men to lay down their lives in the vain effort to accomplish what, humanly speaking, could not be done.   That is true ; and, as Lee is said to have once remarked in another connexion, ' Even as poor a soldier as I am can generally discover mistakes after it is all over '. After Gettysburg was over, like Frederick at Ku- nersdorf and Napoleon at Waterloo, Lee doubtless discovered his mistake.   It was a very simple one : he undervalued his opponent.   The temper of his own weapon he knew ; he made no mistake there.   His mistake lay in his estimate of his antagonist : but that estimate again was based on his own recent experience elsewhere.

On the other hand, from the day I rode over the field of Gettysburg immediately following the fight to that which now is, I have fully and most potently believed that only some disorganized fragments of Lee's army should after that battle have found their way back to Virginia.   The war should have collapsed within sixty days thereafter.   For eighteen hours after the repulse of Pickett's division, I have always felt, and now feel, the fate of the Army of Virginia was as much in General Meade's hands as was the fate of the army led by Napoleon in the hands of Blücher on the night of Waterloo.   As an aggressive force, the Con- federate army was fought out.   It might yet put forth a fierce defensive effort ; it was sure to die game : but

it was impotent for attack. Meade had one entire
corps—perhaps his best—the Sixth, commanded by
Sedgwick, intact. Held in reserve, it had been
divided in support of points deemed weak in the line
of battle. Its reconcentration under its proper commander would at most, however, have been but a
matter of hours. By the early morn of the morrow
following Pickett's repulse, Sedgwick at the head of
a reunited command could have been pressing hard
on the heels of the cavalry, endangering Lee's line of
retreat. The true counter-movement for the fourth
day of continuous fighting would then on Meade's part
have been an exact reversal of Lee's own plan of
battle for the third day. That plan, as described by
Fitzhugh Lee, was simple. 'His (Lee's) purpose was
to turn the enemy's left flank with his First Corps,
and, after the work began there, to demonstrate
against his lines with the others in order to prevent
the threatened flank from being reinforced; these
demonstrations to be converted into a real attack as
the flanking wave of battle rolled over the troops in
their front.' What Lee thus proposed for Meade's
army on the third day, Meade should unquestionably
have returned on Lee's army upon the fourth day.
Sedgwick's corps, following close on a concentrated
cavalry advance, should then have assailed Lee's right
and rear. I once, long afterwards, asked a leading
Confederate general [1], who had been in the very thick
of it on Gettysburg's crucial third day, what would

---

[1] General E. P. Alexander, Chief of Artillery of the corps
commanded by General Longstreet.

have been the outcome had Meade, within two hours of the repulse of Pickett, ordered Sedgwick to get his corps together, and, as soon as he could so do, to move off to the left, occupying Lee's line of retreat. The Confederate right being thus threatened, a general advance would have been in order. The answer I received was immediate : ' Without question we would have been destroyed. We all that night fully expected it ; and could not understand next day why we were unmolested. My ammunition '—for he was an officer of artillery—' would have sufficed but for one short day's fighting more.'

But in all this, as in every speculation of the sort— and the history of warfare is replete with them—the ' if ' is much in evidence ; as much in evidence, indeed, as it is in a certain familiar Shakespearian disquisition. I here introduce what I have said on this topic simply to illustrate what may be described as the balance of miscarriages inseparable from warfare. On the other hand, the manner in which Lee met disaster at Gettysburg—the combination of serene courage and consequent skill with which he extricated his army from its critical situation, commands admiration. I would here say nothing depreciatory of General Meade. He was an accomplished officer as well as a brave soldier. Placed suddenly in a most trying position— assigned to chief command when battle was already joined—untried in his new sphere of action, and caught unprepared, he fought at Gettysburg a stubborn, gallant fight. A good soldier and a skilful commander, a man of character, after he assumed command of the Army of the Potomac, though confronted by its old opponent, serious disaster did not again befall it. Subsequently, he deserved more considerate treatment than he received. With chances at the beginning heavily against him, he saved the crucial day: none the less, as I have already pointed out, I fully believe that, on the fourth of July at Gettysburg, Meade had but firmly to close his hand, and the Army of Northern Virginia was crushed. Perhaps under all the circumstances it was too much to have expected of him; certainly it was not done. Then Lee in turn did avail himself of his opportunity. Skilfully, proudly though sullenly, preserving an unbroken front, he withdrew to Virginia. That withdrawal was masterly.

Of the subsequent campaign, Lee's last—that carried on in the Virginian Wilderness and before and around Richmond during the terrible months between April 1864 and April 1865,—of that campaign I do not, a participant in it, like to talk. It is a hideous and heart-rending memory. I will only say that, contending, with ever diminishing resources both of men and munitions, including food and clothing, against a vastly superior force, Lee fully sustained the great reputation he before had won. Far more successful than Napoleon in his campaign of 1813, and fully as much outnumbered, striking terrible aggressive blows and then, on the defensive, foiling every counter-move of his unrelenting opponent, he there did I believe all that was possible with such means as were at his command. Of the strategy and tactics of those opposed to him in

that titanic grapple I have expressed myself elsewhere, and shall not here speak. Suffice it to say,
Lee held his opponent far more successfully at bay
than did Napoleon the allies before and at Leipsic in
1813, and during the succeeding months which witnessed the closing in upon him at Paris.

> Victrix causa deis placuit, sed victa Catoni.

The personal equation here also must be taken into
the account—remains always to be reckoned with.
Lee, it must be remembered, when, at Chancellorsville, Jackson fell, lost his right arm in battle. That
loss never was made good. Thereafter he remained
maimed. To what extent results would have been
affected, and proved other than history has recorded,
had 'Stonewall' been at Lee's side in the Gettysburg
campaign and in the Wilderness, it would be idle to consider. As a participant on the ultimately winning side,
I can only say I am now glad that thunderbolt of war
was then no longer at Lee's command. I can bear
witness that on one momentous occasion at least, had
'Stonewall' been there in place of him who succeeded to
'Stonewall's' command, I have never been able to see
how a great and apparently irreparable disaster to the
Union cause could have been averted. But I cannot
here enter into details; the incident is of record.
I can only say it was bad enough as it was; and the
individual factor absent!

Narrowly escaping destruction at Gettysburg, my
next contention is that Lee and the Army of Northern
Virginia never sustained defeat. Finally, it is true,
succumbing to exhaustion, to the end they were not

overthrown in fight. And here I approach a large topic, but one closely interwoven with Lee's military career; in fact, as I see it, the explanation of what finally occurred. What then was it that brought about the collapse of the Army of Northern Virginia, and the consequent downfall of the Confederacy? The literature of the War of Secession now constitutes a library in itself. Especially is this true of it in its military aspects. The shelves are crowded with memoirs and biographies of its generals, the stories of its campaigns, the records and achievements of its armies, its army corps, and its regiments. Yet I make bold to say that no well and philosophically considered narrative of the struggle has yet appeared; nor has any satisfactory or comprehensive explanation been given of its extraordinary and unanticipated outcome. Let me briefly set it forth as I see it; only by so doing can I explain what I mean.

Tersely put, dealing only with outlines, the Southern community in 1861 precipitated a conflict on the slavery issue, in implicit reliance on its own warlike capacity and resources, the extent and very defensible character of its territory, and, above all, on its complete control of cotton as the great staple textile fabric of modern civilization. But with this topic I have sufficiently dealt in a previous lecture.

As to a maritime blockade of the South, shutting it up to die of inanition, the idea was believed to be chimerical. That no such feat of maritime force ever had been accomplished, was incontrovertible; nor was it deemed possible of accomplishment now. I have

quoted Confederate utterances of high authority to
this effect. To 'talk of putting up a wall of fire
around eight hundred and fifty thousand square
miles', situated as the Confederacy was, with its twelve
thousand miles of sea-coast, was pronounced too
'absurd' for serious discussion. But, even supposing
it were possible of accomplishment, the doing it
would but the more effectively play the Confederate
game. It would compel intervention. As well shut
off bread from the manufacturing centres of Europe
as stop their supply of cotton. In any or either
event, and in any contingency which might arise,
the victory of the Confederacy was assured. And
this theory of the situation and its outcome was, as
I have already pointed out, accepted by the Southern
community as indisputable.

What occurred? In each case that which had been
pronounced impossible of occurrence. On land the
Confederacy had an ample force of men; they swarmed
to the standards; and no better or more reliable
fighting material was ever gathered together. Well
and skilfully marshalled, the Confederate soldier did
on the march and in battle all that needed to be done.
Nor, so far as the land array was concerned, were
the two sides unequally matched. As Lee with his
instinctive military sense put it, even in the closing
stages of the struggle 'the proportion of experienced
troops is larger in our army than in that of the enemy,
while his numbers exceed our own.' And in warfare
experience, combined with an advantageous defensive,
counts for a great deal. This was so throughout the

conflict; and yet the Confederate cause sank in failure. It did so, moreover, to the complete surprise of a bewildered world. How was this wholly unexpected actual outcome brought about? The simple answer is:—The Confederacy collapsed from inanition! Suffering such occasional reverses and defeats as are incidental to all warfare, it was never crushed in battle or on the field at large until its strength was sapped away by want of food. It died of exhaustion—starved and gasping!

Take a living organism, whatever it may be, place it in a vessel hermetically sealed, and attach to that vessel an air-pump. Set that pump in action; you know what follows. It is needless to describe it. No matter how strong or fierce or self-confident it may be, the victim dies; growing weaker by degrees, it finally collapses. That was the exact condition and fate of the Confederacy. What had been confidently pronounced impossible was done. Steam put in its work, and the Confederacy was sealed up within itself by the blockade. Operations in the field then acted as an air-pump, the exhausting character of which could not be exceeded. On the other hand, the wellnigh complete exclusion of Southern cotton from the manufacturing centres of Europe did not cause revolution there, nor compel intervention here. Man's foresight once more came to grief. As is apt to be the case, the unexpected occurred.

Thus the two decisive defeats of the Confederacy—those which really brought about its downfall and compelled Lee to surrender the army under his command—were inflicted not before Vicksburg, nor yet in

Virginia, not in the field at all : they were sustained, the one, almost by default, on the ocean ; the other, most fatal of all, after sharpest struggle in Lancashire.

The supremacy of the Union on the ocean was involved in the issue of the Lancashire struggle; and upon ocean supremacy depended every considerable land operation of the Union armies: the retention by the National Government of New Orleans, when once captured, and the consequent control of the Mississippi ; Sherman's great march to the sea; his subsequent movement through the Carolinas; Grant's operations before Petersburg; generally, the maintenance of the national armies in the field. It is in fact no exaggeration to assert that both the conception and the carrying out of every large Union operation of the war, without a single exception, hinged and depended on complete national maritime or water supremacy. It is equally indisputable that the struggle in Lancashire was decisive of that supremacy. As Lee himself asserted in the death agony of the Confederacy, he had never believed it could in the long run make good its independence 'unless foreign powers should, directly or indirectly, assist' it in so doing. Thus, strange as it sounds, it follows as a logical consequence that Lee and his Army of Northern Virginia were first reduced to inanition, and finally compelled to succumb, as the result of events on the other side of the Atlantic, largely stimulated by a moral impulse they were powerless to counteract.

It is curious, at times almost comical, to trace histo-

rical parallels. Plutarch is, of course, the standard
exemplar of that sort of treatment. Among other
great careers, Plutarch, as every college boy knows,
tells the story of King Pyrrhus, the Epirot. A great
captain, Pyrrhus devised a military formation which
his opponents could not successfully face, and his
career was consequently one of victory. But at last
he met his fate. Assaulting the town of Argos, he
became entangled in its streets; and, fighting his way
out, he was killed, struck down by a tile thrown from
a house-top by an Argive woman.[1] The Confederacy,
and through the Confederacy Lee, underwent a not
dissimilar fate; for, as an historical fact, it was a
missile from a woman's hand which was decisive
of that Lancashire conflict, and so doomed the Confederacy. Though one was a fragment of roofing and
the other a book, the missiles were equally fatal.

---

[1] An almost identical experience is recounted in scriptural
narrative as having fallen to the lot of Abimelech, son of Gideon,
in his assault upon Thebez:—

51 But there was a strong tower within the city, and thither
fled all the men and women, and all they of the city, and shut it
to them, and gat them up to the top of the tower.

52 And Abimelech came unto the tower, and fought against it,
and went hard unto the door of the tower to burn it with fire.

53 And a certain woman cast a piece of a millstone upon
Abimelech's head, and all to brake his skull.

54 Then he called hastily unto the young man his armour-
bearer, and said unto him, Draw thy sword, and slay me, that
men say not of me, A woman slew him. And his young man
thrust him through, and he died.

55 And when the men of Israel saw that Abimelech was dead,
they departed every man unto his place.

Judges ix.

The difference was of time, and changed conditions. There elapsed between the two events two thousand one hundred and thirty years, during which the world had moved considerably.

Foreign intervention being thus withheld, and the control of the sea by the Union made absolute, the blockade was gradually perfected. The fateful process then went steadily on. Armies might be resisted in the field ; the working of the air-pump could not be stopped. And, day and night, season after season, the air-pump worked. So the atmosphere of the Confederacy became more and more attenuated ; respiration sensibly harder. Air-hole on air-hole was closed. First, New Orleans fell ; then Vicksburg, and the Mississippi flowed free ; next, Sherman, securely counting on the control of the sea as a base of new operations on land, penetrated the vitals of the Confederacy ; then, relying still on maritime co-operation, he pursued his almost unopposed way through the Carolinas : while Grant, with his base secure upon the James river and Fortress Monroe, beleagured Richmond. Lee with his Army of Northern Virginia calmly, but watchfully and resolutely, confronted him. The Confederate lines were long and thin, guarded by poorly clad and half-fed men. But, veterans, they held their assailants firmly at bay. As Lee, however, fully realized, it was only a question of time. The working of the air-pump was beyond his sphere either of influence or operations. Nothing could stop it.

Viewed in a half-century's perspective, the situation was simply and manifestly impossible of continuance.

To it there could be but one outcome. Wilmington, the single sea-port of North Carolina, was also the last haven remaining to the blockade-runner. Fort Fisher, constructed as Wilmington's harbour defence, commanded its approach. On January 16, 1865, the telegraph flashed tidings that, as the result of combined naval and military Union operations, Fort Fisher had fallen. Its fall thus closed the South's single remaining air-hole. But though the sealing was now hermetical, the air-pump still kept on in its deadly, silent work.

Three months later the long-delayed inevitable occurred. The collapse came. The only legitimate cause of surprise is, that under such conditions it should have been so long deferred. That adversity is the test of man is a commonplace; that Lee and his Army of Northern Virginia were during the long, dragging winter of 1864-5 most direfully subjected to that test, need not here be said, any more than it is needful to say that they bore the test manfully. But the handwriting was on the wall; the men were taxed beyond the limits of human endurance. And Lee knew it. 'Yesterday, the most inclement day of the winter,' he reported on February 8, 1865, the right wing of his army 'had to be retained in line of battle, having been in the same condition the two previous days and nights.... Under these circumstances, heightened by assaults and fire of the enemy, some of the men had been without meat for three days, and all were suffering from reduced rations and scant clothing, exposure to battle, cold, hail, and sleet. . . . The physical strength of the men, if their courage survives, must fail under this treatment.' If it was so with the men, with the animals it was even worse. 'Our cavalry', he added, 'has to be dispersed for want of forage.' Even thus Lee's army faced an opponent vastly superior in numbers, whose ranks were being constantly replenished ; a force armed, clothed, equipped, fed and sheltered as no similar force in the world's history had ever been before. I state only indisputable facts. Lee proved equal to even this occasion. Bearing a bold, confident front, he was serene and outwardly calm ; alert, resourceful, formidable to the last, individually he showed no sign of weakness, not even occasional petulance. Inspired by his example, the whole South seemed to lean up against him in implicit, loving reliance. The tribute was superlative.

Finally, when in April the summons to conflict came, the Army of Northern Virginia, the single remaining considerable organized force of the Confederacy, seemed to stagger to its feet; and, gaunt and grim, shivering with cold and emaciated with hunger, worn down by hard unceasing attrition, it faced its enemy, formidable still. As I have since studied that situation, listened to the accounts of Confederate officers active in the closing movements, and read the letters written me by those of the rank and file, it has seemed as if Lee's command then cohered and moved by mere force of habit. Those composing it failed to realize the utter hopelessness of the situation—the disparity of the conflict. I am sure Jefferson Davis failed to realize it ; so, I think, in less degree, did Lee. They talked, for instance, of recruits, and of a levy in mass. Lee counselled the arming of the slaves; and when, after Lee had surrendered, Davis on the 10th of April, 1865, held his last war conference at Greensboro', he was still confident he would in a few weeks have another army in the field, and did not hesitate to express his faith that 'we can whip the enemy yet, if our people will turn out.' I have often pondered over what Davis had in mind when he ventured this opinion : or what led Lee to advocate the enlistment of negroes. Both were soldiers; and, besides being great in his profession, Lee was more familiar than any other man alive with actual conditions then existing in the Confederate camps. Both Davis and Lee, therefore, must have known that, in those final stages of the conflict, if the stamp of a foot upon the ground would have brought a million men into the field, the cause of the Confederacy would thereby have been in no wise strengthened; on the contrary, what was already bad would have been made much worse. For, to be effective in warfare, men must be fed and clothed and armed. Organized in commands, they must have rations as well as ammunition, commissary and quartermaster trains, artillery horses and forage. In the closing months of the Civil War both Lee and Davis knew perfectly well that they could not arm, nor feed, nor clothe, nor transport the forces already in the field; they were without money, and the soldiers most inadequately supplied with arms, clothing, quartermaster or medical supplies, commissariat or ammunition. Notoriously, those then on the muster-rolls were going home, or deserting to the enemy, as the one alternative to death from privation —hunger and cold. If then, a million, or even only a poor hundred thousand fresh recruits had in answer to the summons swarmed to the lines around Richmond, how would it have bettered the situation? An organized army is a mighty consumer of food and material; and food and material have to be served out to it every day. They must be supplied as regularly as the sun rises and sets. And the organized resources of the Confederacy were exhausted; its ports were in the hands of the enemy or hermetically sealed; its granaries—Georgia and the valley of the Shenandoah—were notoriously devastated and desolate; its lines of communication and supply were cut, or in the hands of the invader.

Realizing this, Lee, when the time was ripe, rose to the full height of the great occasion. The value of Character made itself felt. The service Lee now rendered to the common country, the obligation under which he placed his fellow countrymen, whether of the North or South, has not, I think, been always appreciated; and to overstate it would be difficult.

That the situation in the Confederacy was at that juncture to the last degree critical is matter of history. Further organized resistance was impossible. The means for it did not exist; could not be had. Cut off completely from the outer world, the South had consumed itself, its vitals were impaired. The single alternative to surrender was disbandment and irregular

warfare. As General Joseph E. Johnston, at the close
of the war esteemed, next to Lee, the ablest Confederate commander, subsequently wrote, ' Without the
means of purchasing supplies of any kind, or procur-
ing or repairing arms, we could continue the war only
as robbers or guerillas.' But that it should be so
continued was wholly possible; nay more, it was in
the line of precedent—it had been done before, and
more than once. It has since been done, notably in
South Africa. It was, moreover, the course advocated
by many Southern participants in the struggle as that
proper to be pursued; and that it would be pursued
was accepted as of course by all foreign observers and
by the organ of the Confederacy in London. ' A
strenuous resistance and not surrender', the *Index*
declared, ' was the unalterable determination of the
Confederate authorities.'

Indeed, had the veil over the immediate future then
been lifted, the outrages, and humiliations worse than
outrage, of the period of so-called reconstruction but
actual servile domination, now to ensue, revealed
itself, no room for doubt exists that the dread alternative would have been adopted. Even as it was, the
scales hung trembling. Anything or everything was
possible; even that pistol shot of the crazed theatrical
fool which five days after the meeting of Grant and
Lee at Appomattox so irretrievably complicated a
delicate and dangerous situation. None the less, what
Lee and Grant had done on April 9th could not be
wholly undone even by the deed in Ford's theatre of
April 14th. Much had been secured. Of that April 9

and what then occurred, I do not care to speak; for I feel I could not speak adequately or in words sufficiently simple. But, in my judgement, there is not in our American history any incident more creditable to our manhood, or so indicative of a racial possession of Character. Marked throughout by a straightforward dignity of personal bearing and responsibility in action, Appomattox was marred by no touch of the theatrical, no effort at posturing. I know not to which of the two leaders, there face to face, preference should be given. They were thoroughly typical; the one of Illinois and the New West, the other of Virginia and the Old Dominion. Grant was considerate and magnanimous— restrained in victory; Lee, dignified in defeat, carried himself with that simple fitness which compelled respect. Verily, 'he that ruleth his spirit is better than he that taketh a city!'

The lead that day given by Lee proved decisive of the course to be pursued by his Confederate fellows in arms. At first, and for a brief space, there was in the councils of the Southern leaders much diversity of opinion as to what should or could be done. Calm and dignified in presence of overwhelming disaster, the voice of Jefferson Davis was that of Milton's 'Scepter'd king',—'My sentence is for open war!' Lee was not there; none the less, Lee, absent, prevailed over Davis. The sober second thought satisfied all but the most extreme that what Lee had done they best might do. Thus the die was cast. And now, forty-eight years after the event, it is appalling to reflect what in all human probability would have re-

sulted had the election then been other than it was—had
Lee's personality and character not intervened.   The
struggle had lasted four full years ; the assassination
of Lincoln was as oil on the Union fire.   With a million men, inured to war, on the national muster rolls,
men impatient of further resistance, accustomed to
licence and now educated up to the belief that War
was Hell, and that the best way to bring it to
a close was to intensify Hell—with such a force as this
to reckon with, made more reckless in brutality by the
assassin's senseless shot, the Confederacy need have
looked for no consideration, no mercy.   Visited by
the besom of destruction, it would have been harried
out of existence.   Fire and sword sweeping over it,
what the sword spared the fire would have consumed.
Whether such an outcome of a prolonged conflict—a
conflict prolonged as more recently was that in South
Africa—would in its result have been more morally in-
jurious to the North than it would have been destructive
materially to the South, is not now to be considered.   It
would, however, assuredly have come about.

From that crown of sorrows Lee saved the common
country.   He was the one man in the Confederacy
who could exercise decisive influence.   It was the
night of the 8th of April, lacking ten days only of
exactly four full years—years very full for us who lived
through them—since the not dissimilar night when
Lee had paced the floor at Arlington.   Then, he was
communing with himself over the fateful issue between State and Nation, an issue forced upon him.
A decision of even greater import was now to be

reached, and reached by him. A commander of the usual cast would under such circumstances have sought advice—perhaps support; at least, a divided responsibility. Even though himself by nature and habit a masterful man and one accustomed to direct, he would have called a council, and hearkened to those composing it. This Lee did not do. Singularly self-poised, he sought no external aid ; but, sitting before his bivouac fire at Appomattox, he reviewed the situation. Doing so, as before at Arlington, he reached his own conclusion. That conclusion he himself at the time expressed in words, brief, indeed, but vibrating with moral triumph : ' The question is—Is it right to surrender this army ? If it is right, then I will take all the responsibility.' The conclusion reached at Arlington in the April night of 1861 to some seems to have been wrong, inexcusable even ; all concur in that reached before the Appomattox camp-fire in the April vigils of 1865. Lee then a second time decided ; and he decided right.

His work was done; but from failure he plucked triumph. Thenceforth Lee wore defeat as 'twere a laurel crown. A few days later a small group of horsemen appeared in the morning hours on the farther side of the Richmond pontoons across the James. By some strange intuition it became known that General Lee was of the party ; and, silent and uncovered, a crowd—Virginians all—gathered along the route the horsemen would take. ' There was no excitement, no hurrahing ; but as the great chief passed, a deep, loving murmur, greater than these, rose from the very hearts of the crowd. Taking off his hat, and simply bowing his head, the man great in adversity passed silently to his own door; it closed upon him, and his people had seen him for the last time in his battle harness.'

From the day that he affixed his signature to those 9th of April terms of surrender submitted to him by Grant at Appomattox to the day five years later when he last drew breath at Lexington, Lee's subsequent course was consistent. In his case there was no vacillation, no regretful glances backward thrown.

Five years of life and active usefulness yet remained—years in my judgement most creditable to Lee, the most useful to his country of his whole life; for, during them, he set to Virginia and his own people a high example, an example of lofty character and simple dignified bearing. Uttering no complaints, entering into no controversies, he was as one, in suffering all, that suffers nothing. Blood and judgement were in his case also well commingled; and it so fell out that he accepted Fortune's buffets and rewards with equal thanks. His record and appearance during those final years are pleasant to dwell upon. They reflect honour on American manhood. Turning his face courageously to the future, he uttered no word of repining over the past. Yet his occupation also was gone—

> The royal banner, and all quality,
> Pride, pomp, and circumstance of glorious war!

But with Lee this did not imply, as with the noble Moor,

> Farewell the tranquil mind! farewell content.

Far from it; for as the gates closed on the old occupation, they opened on a new. And it was an occupation through which he gave to his country, north and south, a priceless gift.

Indifferent to wealth, he was scrupulous as respects those money dealings a carelessness in regard to which has embittered the lives of so many public men, as not infrequently it has tarnished their fame. Lee's whole career will be scrutinized in vain for a suggestion even of the sordid, or of an obligation he failed to meet. He was nothing if not self-respecting. He once wrote to a member of his family, ' "vile dross" has never been a drug with me,' yet his generosity as a giver from his narrow means was limited only by his resources. Restricting his own wants to necessities, he contributed, to an extent which excites surprise, to both public calls and private needs. But the most priceless of those contributions were contained in the precepts he in those closing years inculcated, and in the unconscious example he set.

And at this point I for the present part with Lee; but in so doing I revert to Burke's words: 'Great men are the guideposts and landmarks in the State'. Is Lee entitled to be numbered among the American World-Great? to constitute an additional star in that as yet not numerous galaxy? General, Educator, Virginian, by some of my countrymen Lee is still looked upon as a traitor and denounced as a renegade; by yet others he is venerated and loved—I might even say idolized. Here in Oxford, that ancient seat of old-world learning, I, an American, am simply presenting

Lee's credentials on which to base his possible admis-
sion among the World's Great—one more American
Immortal. In the case of Lee, as in that of Verulam,
to pass finally upon this is a function reserved to
' foreign nations and the next ages '.

My course of lectures now draws to its appointed
end. Before closing it, however, I propose to de-
vote the few minutes remaining to another subject,
one very cognate to Lee and the attitude assumed by
him at the close of the war in which he bore so conspicuous a part. And here, as an American speaking
under the auspices of a British University, and that
University Oxford, I am conscious of entering on
somewhat delicate, perhaps I might even say dangerous ground. Nevertheless, the topic, one of great
historical interest, has, also, a very immediate connexion with a process of historic development of
which I treated in my first lecture—I refer of course
to that American form of local self-government known
by us as State Sovereignty.

You here in Great Britain have for years, I might
even say for generations, been wrestling with what
you call the Irish Question ; for, as we in America
have sufficient cause to realize, Ireland has through
centuries been a restless, discontented, and at times
unruly portion of the United Kingdom. It is so still ;
and you are now considering, and propose apparently
soon to enact into your constitutional law a measure
of what you designate Home Rule. Now, at the outset,
let me say I am not here to discuss situations I at best

only very imperfectly understand, or to hold myself
out as one either qualified or disposed to instruct
Englishmen, much less Irishmen, on their interests,
their policies, or the principles of sound polity or constitutional law and usage involved in the issues now
in debate.   I fully appreciate the fact that institutions
differ; and the experience of one community may
have no application to conditions existing in another,
even though the two may speak the same tongue and
trace a common descent.   Moreover, in the case of
nationalities as in that of individuals, the pathological
fact holds true that what is food to the one may be
poison to the other.   All this I premise; and so, what
I have now to say may or may not be applicable to
the situation by which you find yourselves confronted;
nevertheless our recent experience bears some resemblance to your present situation, and may be worth
considering in connexion therewith.   For we too at
the close of our Civil War found ourselves with a race
issue on our hands and a section of our common
country seething with discontent—in a word, per-
plexed in the extreme by a condition of great unrest.

Our War of Secession closed in April, 1865, with
the complete submission of the States which had composed the Confederacy.   Falling by the hand of an
assassin in the very hour of victory, Abraham Lincoln
had been succeeded in the presidential chair by Andrew
Johnson.   Verily, a most unfortunate substitution!
Of neither is it necessary for me to speak; but,
historically, there followed a period on the events and
outcome of which Americans do not like to dwell.

Properly and intelligently studied, however, it conveys a lesson—possibly a lesson applicable in some degree to your British conditions of to-day.

Because, as the outcome of our War of Secession, and as penalty for what was done by individuals in the course thereof, no blood flowed on the scaffold and no confiscations of houses or lands marked the close of the struggle, it has always been assumed by us of the victorious party that extreme, indeed unprecedented, clemency was shown to the vanquished; and that, subsequently, they had no good ground of complaint or sufficient cause for restiveness. That history will accord assent to this somewhat self-complacent conviction is open to question. On the contrary, it may not unfairly be doubted whether a people prostrate after civil conflict has often received severer measure than was dealt out to the so-called reconstructed Confederate States during the years immediately succeeding the close of strife. Adam Smith somewhere defined rebels and heretics as 'those unlucky persons who, when things have come to a certain degree of violence, have the misfortune to be of the weaker party.' Spoliation and physical suffering have immemorially been their lot. The Confederate, it is true, when he ceased to resist, escaped this visitation in its usual and time-approved form. Nevertheless, he was by no means exempt from it. In the matter of confiscation, it has been computed that the freeing of the slaves by act of war swept out of existence property valued at some four hundred millions sterling; while, over and above this, a system of simultaneous reconstruction subjected the disfranchised master to the rule of the enfranchised bondsman. For a community conspicuously masterful, and notoriously quick to resent affront, to be thus placed by alien force under the civil rule of those of a different and distinctly inferior race, only lately their bondsmen and property, is not physical torment, it is true, but that it is mild or considerate treatment can hardly be contended. Yet this—slave confiscation and reconstruction under African rule—was the war penalty imposed on the States of the Confederacy. That the policy inspired at the time a feeling of bitter resentment in the South was no cause for wonder. Upon it time has already recorded a verdict. Following the high precedent set at Appomattox, it was distinctly unworthy. Conceived in passion, it ignored both science and the philosophy of statesmanship; worse yet, it was ungenerous. Lee, for instance, again setting the example, applied formally for amnesty and a restoration of civil rights within two months of his surrender. His application was silently ignored; while he died ' a prisoner on parole ', the suffrage denied him was conferred on his manumitted slaves. Verily, it was not alone ' the base Judian ' of the olden time who ' threw a pearl away richer than all his tribe ! '

The course thus adopted led to its natural results — a deep feeling of wrong, of deprivation and resentment pervaded the entire region which had constituted the Confederacy. It manifested itself in a spirit of restlessness, in acts of violence, and in outrages on individuals. This was only some forty years ago; to-day peace, concord, and good-fellowship reign throughout the common country. Slavery has ceased to exist; the Lost Cause is a cherished memory—a sentiment: there is no more loyal and contented portion of the Union than those States which fifty years back consti- tuted the Confederacy. Through what means was this extraordinary transmutation worked? By what process was it brought about?

Strange indeed as it sounds, the remedy for the ills consequent to the war was found in a recourse to the system which had caused it. As I endeavoured to point out in the first lecture of my course, the prin- ciple of State Sovereignty applied in its extreme form in practice led to the trouble; but, fifteen years later, that same principle of State Sovereignty in its proper form, now known as Local Self-Government, or, in other words, Home Rule, brought to a close the unrest and disturbance which naturally ensued from the strife. Operating as a charm, it worked a miracle.

In this result, historically complete in our case, is there a lesson beneficially to be studied by Great Britain in disposing of the issues long and still con- fronting it in Ireland? I do not know; nor would it be for me to express an opinion on that head did I hold one. But, of course, it would at once be objected that with us no racial question embittered the debate, or was involved in the solution of the problem—no Celt was arrayed against Saxon. Perhaps not; but, on the other hand, evidence of eminent foreign witnesses stands recorded—among others that of Lord Wolseley, and that of Russell, your *Times*

Crimean War correspondent, both speaking from careful personal observation—that the hate of Celt to Saxon, and the contempt of Saxon for Celt, simply paled and grew expressionless when compared with the contempt and hate felt by the Southron towards the Yankee anterior to our Civil War and while it was in progress. No Houyhnhnms ever looked on Yahoo with greater aversion; better, far better death than further contamination through political association. This was only fifty years since; it is all over now, ancient and forgotten history; even discredited as such, pronounced unveracious! Yet it is susceptible of proof.

But again it will obviously be objected that we of the North did not have in the Confederacy a colony, settlement, or community of our own people whom it would be a baseness to desert—in fact, a Southern Ulster. But this again is hardly so—we did have such a community, and it numbered millions; the Africans, once slaves, we had emancipated and were in honour bound to protect. And this argument was used to its full extent—passionately even, and for a time effectively, in opposition to the growing sentiment in favour of local self-government, a recurrence to State Sovereignty. None the less, the thing ultimately came about; wearied with unrest, complete Home Rule was in 1877, twelve years after the close of the war, conceded to South Carolina, the prolific mother of discord, and last of the Confederacy to have statehood restored to it.

What resulted? Every political issue, every step

in the process of political evolution, be the same upward or downward, is a question of *pro* and *con*, a balancing of advantages. Sometimes, and not infrequently as we all know, it of necessity becomes a balancing of public and general good against private hardship and individual wrong. As an abstract proposition, however, subject of course to proper limitations, the general public good is the end to be kept in view. Applying now this principle to the concrete case of the emancipated African—our Ulster—there is no question he suffered hardship when Home Rule was restored to the States once constituting the Confederacy. Deprived of the franchise in open disregard of the fundamental law enacted for his protection in it, throughout large sections of the common country he was not, nor is he now, practically the equal of the white in presence of the law. I state the case to its full extent, and in the baldest way. But, on the other hand, general peace, goodwill and loyalty were restored; throughout the land unrest ceased. Where under such circumstances do we look for the balance in the weighing of the *pros* and *cons*?

But on this head I wish to be more than fair; so I will state the Ulster argument, the wanton—if you desire so to stigmatize it—abandonment to a cruel oppressor of those we were bound to protect. As a nation we were under the deepest obligations to the Afro-American. I do not care again to summon from his forgotten grave Mr. Peacock, once member of Parliament for North Essex, with his confident visions of Jacqueries and massacres of Cawnpore surely to result

Z

from any attempt to make effective Lincoln's Proclamation of Emancipation. A very foolish man, let him and the many who talked as he talked rest in their wonted oblivion. To exhume and gibbet them now would be ungenerous; almost cruel, it savours of the ghoulish. The plain historic truth, however, is that African slavery, as it existed in the United States anterior to 1862, an evil institution at best, yet constituted a mild form of servitude, as servitude then existed and immemorially had almost everywhere existed. And this was incontrovertibly proven by the course of events subsequent to the issue of the Proclamation. Before 1862, it was confidently believed that any open social agitation within, or violent disturbance from without, would inevitably lead to a Southern servile insurrection. As I have already elsewhere shown, the Proclamation when first issued was denounced almost universally and in no measured terms. It was stigmatized as a measure unwarranted in warfare. From its practical operation unimaginable horrors would surely ensue.

What actually occurred is now historic. The confident anticipations of our English brethren were, not for the first time, negatived; nor is there any page in our American record more creditable to those concerned than the attitude held by the African during the fierce internecine struggle which prevailed between April, 1861, and April, 1865. In it there is scarcely a trace, if indeed there is any trace at all, of such a condition of affairs as had developed in the Antilles in 1790 and in Hindustan in 1850. The attitude of the African towards his Confederate owner was submissive and kindly. Although the armed and masterful domestic protector was at the front and engaged in deadly, all-absorbing conflict, yet the women and children of the Southern plantation, with unbarred doors, slept free from apprehension, much more from molestation. This record certainly entitled the emancipated bonds-man to much consideration at the hands of those who had emancipated him. An obligation had been assumed. Yet it is an undeniable historical fact that before the memories of the Civil War had yet ceased to be vivid, the emancipated Afro-American was, under the operation of a restored State Sovereignty—as you would call it, Home Rule—left to the far from tender mercies of his quondam owner. It certainly looked bad. The possible outcome of such a proceeding was foreseen, and to a very considerable extent it came about. Yet, in the not remote close the Afro-American himself was greatly benefited. Ceasing to be a bone of contention and an object of political dislike—in a word, a scape-goat—he shared not least of all in the results of a restored good feeling. In other words, left alone he found his place, and, in a measure, learned to protect himself. The problem of the advance and present condition of those of the African race in what was once their land of bondage is with us in America much debated and involved in doubt. Into it, though most interesting, I do not propose here to enter. It is unquestionably one of the numerous great issues, as yet only partially solved and not become historical, resulting from the outcome of our War of Secession.   On one point, however, no question remains : it has passed out of the forum of political discussion.   There is an ancient and not altogether savoury precept as to the cure to be attained by the ministering to a patient of a hair of the dog that bit him ; and so in America, looking fifty years later at the ultimate solution of the troubles incident to the outcome of our civil strife—and they were many and great—no question exists, North or South, among white or black as to the balance of advantage or disadvantage resulting from the restoration after the close of our contest of Home Rule, under the guise of a limited State Sovereignty, to the several communities once composing the Confederate States of America. In all the United States not one man, I make bold to assert, could be found gravely and dispassionately to advocate a recurrence to the policy of force and repression to which a mistaken recourse was had during the brief and discredited decennium between 1866 and 1876.

Is it not within the bounds of possibility that, intelligently observed and dispassionately studied, there might here again be found for Great Britain of to-day a suggestive moral derivable from trans-Atlantic historical solidarity ?

INDEX

Abimelech, death of, 159 n.

Achaian league, 36.

Acton, John Emerich Ward Dalberg, Baron, on Lee, 141.

Adams, Charles Francis, self-command as American Minister, 18; anxieties, 102, 104.

Air-pump, blockade as, 157, 160.

Albert, Francis Charles Augustus Emmanuel, Prince Consort, fear of Democracy, 22.

Alexander, E. P., 151.

Alien and sedition laws, 41.

Allegiance, 46; Lee and, 136.

America, Burke on, 33; celebrities, 134.

Appomattox, 32; surrender of Lee, 165.

Arbitration, Geneva, 121.

Argyll, Duke of, 18, 78

Armada, Spanish, 16.

Army, Southern, 156; of Virginia, last stand, 161.

Articles of Confederation, 39.

Ashworth, Henry, on cost of cotton, 123.

Asia, cotton of, 90, 122.

Bacon, Francis, Lord, 171.

Bank of England and cotton, 66.

Bathurst, Henry, Burke's vision, 33.

Bentinck, G. W., on Democracy, 109.

Beresford-Hope, Alexander James, on Proclamation of Emancipation, 108.

Bernhardi, Friedrich von, on English policy in American War, 57, 112, 117.

Blackburn, cotton famine, 89.

Blackwood's Edinburgh Magazine, on Conservatism, 21; on American characteristic, 126.

Blockade of South, believed impossible, 64; and cotton, 67, 88; effective, 155.

Bright, John, Democrat, 22; supports the north, 70, 77, 84; influence, 78; prophecy, 88; Proclamation of Emancipation, 111.

Brougham, Henry, Lord, 119.

Browning, Robert, 84.

Bryan, William Jennings, 28.

Bryce, James, on American War of Secession, 10.

Burke, Edmund, vision of America, 33; on great men, 133.

Burnside, Ambrose Everett, 21, 145.

Cabinet, British, meeting on mediation, 99, 103, 107; collectivity, 104.

California, legislation against Asiatics, 27, 51.

Carlyle, Thomas, 119.

Chancellorsville, 144.

Charles I, 30.

Chatham, Earl of, 36.

Chattel-humanity, end of, 14.

Churchill, John, Duke of Marlborough, 142.

Citizenship, 46, 53.

Cobden, Richard, 78, 92; on Lancashire, 95; assurance against intervention, 112.

Coleridge, John Taylor, Great Britain in American War of Secession, 18.

Collectivism, 15.

Colonies discredited, 76.

Common law, 46.

Compromise in Federal Constitution, 38.

Confederacy, Southern, collapse of, 157.

Confederation, New England, 31.

Conservatism, reaction to, in Great Britain, 21.

Constitution, United States, framing of, 37; sovereignty under, 43.

Cooper, Anthony Ashley, Earl of Shaftesbury, 83.

Cotton, supremacy of, 65, 97, 124; and blockade, 67; crisis, 87, 100,

122; American crop, 1860, 88; Asiatic, 90; prices, 91, 122.
Crimea, War of the, 15.

Daily News on Proclamation of Emancipation, 111.
Darwin, Charles, 79.
Davis, Jefferson, 142; desires to continue war, 163, 166.
Declaration of Independence, 36.
Delane, John Thadeus, 75.
De Leon, T. C., 67.
Democracy, movement toward, 14; collapse of, 21; fear of, 72, 109; training, 127.
Derby, Earl of, 92.
Dickens, Charles, 72.
Disraeli, Benjamin, Earl of Beaconsfield, 18, 81; on colonies, 76.
Drake, Sir Francis, 16.
Dred, Mrs. Stowe's, 83.

Fisher, Fort, 161.
Forster, William Edward, 78.
France, American possessions, 76; mediation, 99.
Franklin, Benjamin, 36.
Fredericksburg, 144.

Geneva, arbitration, 121.
George Griswold, relief ship, 95.
Gettysburg campaign, 146.
Gibson, Thomas Milner, 78.
Gladstone, William Ewart, 93; on American Union, 62, 116; mediation, 101, 117; Newcastle speech, 104, 128; distrust of Palmerston, 105; after the war, 115; utterance remembered, 118; Treaty of Washington, 121.
Grant, Ulysses Simpson, 145, 158; at Appomattox, 166.
Granville, George Leveson-Gower, Earl, 102; on Gladstone and Palmerston, 105.
Great Britain, opinion on American War, 11, 18, 58, 69, 71; on Democracy, 21, Great Rebellion, 29; Bernhardi on, 57.
Griswold, George, 95.
Guns, breechloading and magazine, 16.

Hammond, James Henry, power of

South, 63; on blockade, 64; cotton supremacy, 66.
History as a science, 114.
Holmes, Oliver Wendell, 138.
Home Rule in Ireland, 171.
Hooker, Joseph, 145, 149.
Hughes, Thomas, 78.
Hyde, Edward, Earl of Clarendon, 30.

Index, on cotton crisis, 93; Proclamation of Emancipation, 109; no surrender, 165.
India, cotton fortunes, 122.
Intervention, proposed French, 77, 127; Palmerston, 99.
Ireland, Home Rule in, 171.

Jackson, Thomas Jonathan ('Stonewall'), 143, 145, 154.
Japan, legislation of California, 27.
Jefferson, Thomas, 41, 45.
Johnson, Andrew, 172.
Johnston, Joseph Eccleston, 142, 165.

Kentucky Resolutions, 1798, 41, 139.

Lancashire, 68, 70, 158; cotton supply, 89; labour in, 91; patient endurance, 93; relief returns, 96.
Leadership in War of Independence, 36.
Lee, Henry, and Virginia, 139.
Lee, Robert Edward, greatness of, 134, 170; charges against, 135, 138; State influence, 137; choice to follow State, 140; as general, 142; Gettysburg campaign, 146; confidence in army, 149; final campaign, 153, 160; last stand, 161; to arm slaves, 163; surrenders, 166; after the war, 168; indifference to wealth, 170; denied suffrage, 174.
Lepanto, battle of, 16.
Lewis, Sir George Cornewall, 18; reply to Gladstone, 106.
Lincoln, Abraham, 127; Proclamation of Emancipation, 14, 19, 108; *Times* on, 74; assassination, 165.
Long Parliament, 30.
Longstreet, James, 145.
Louisiana, sale by France, 76.

McClellan, George Brinton, 21,145.
Manchester school, 76.
Massachusetts, Constitution of, 36 ; Texas, 42.
Meade, George Gordon, 147, 149, 152.
Mediation, proposed, 100.
Merrimac, 15.
Mill, John Stuart, 78 ; on War of Secession, 19.
Mississippi, control of, 158.
Monitor, 16.
Moore, John Bassett, 53.

Napoleon I, military aphorism, 144.
Napoleon III, 69 ; favours South, 75 ; American ambitions, 76 ; intervention in American war, 77, 100.
Nationality, American, 29 ; not sovereign, 38 ; historical development, 44.
Navy, in War of Secession, 15.
New England Confederation, 1643, 31 ; and embargo, 41.
New Orleans, 158.
North, the, and nationality, 49.
Northcote, Sir Stafford, 18.
Northumberland on Democracy, 23.
Nullification in South Carolina, 42.

Ocean, control of the, 158.
Oxford University, American Lectures, 9 ; cotton relief, 92.

Palmerston, *see* Temple.
Peacock, —, on Proclamation of Emancipation, 108.
Pelleten, Eugene, on cotton supremacy, 124.
Pemberton, John Clifford, 145.
Peter the Hermit, 80.
Petersburg, Va., 158.
Plutarch, history of Pyrrhus, 159.
Pope, John, 145.
' Pope ' campaign, 98.
Potter, Thomas Bayley, 78.
Preston, cotton famine, 89.
Proclamation of Emancipation, 14, 19 ; issue of, 108 ; comments on, 108, 178.
Pyrrhus, death of, 159.

Race hatreds, 175.

Recognition of South proposed, 99.
Reconstruction in South, 165, 173.
Rhodes, James Ford, 9.
Rochdale, meeting in, 94.
Roebuck, John Arthur, 119.
Rousseau, James Jacques, 80.
Russell, John, Earl, 22, 98 ; on recognition of South, 99 ; circular to Cabinet, 100.
Russell, William Howard, 20, 175.
Russia, mediation, 99.

Saturday Review, 19.
Scotland and Mrs. Stowe, 83.
Scott, Winfield, 138.
Sebastopol, naval operations, 16.
Secession, War of, begun, 61 ; Lee on, 137.
Sedgwick, John, 151.
Seward, William Henry, 127 ; instructions to Adams, 102.
Sherman, William Tecumseh, 145, 158.
Slavery, end of human, 14 ; in 1820, 41 ; and sovereignty, 48 ; British against, 72 ; disappearing, 81.
Slavery, in War of Secession, 20.
Slaves, protection of, 176 ; conduct in war, 178.
Smith, Adam, on rebels and heretics, 173.
Smith, Goldwin, 78.
Socialism, 15.
South Carolina and nullification, 42 ; State's rights, 138.
South, the, and State Sovereignty, 49; resources, 62, 69; confidence, 63 ; foreign support, 69 ; cotton, 88.
Sovereignty, State, 96,.136; divided, 43, 47 ; and slavery, 48.
Stanley, Edward George Geoffrey Smith, Earl of Derby, fear of Democracy, 22.
State Sovereignty, 29, 45 ; and Home Rule, 171 ; in South, 174.
State's rights, 40.
Stephen, Leslie, English opinion of America, 18.
Stowe, Harriet Beecher, 68, 77, 93 ; *Uncle Tom's Cabin*, 70, 79, 124 ; European greetings, 82 ; *Dred*, 83.
Suffrage, under reconstruction, 174.

Sutherland, Duke and Duchess of, 83.

Temple, Henry John, Viscount Palmerston, and Delane, 75; proposes intervention, 99, 129; dislike of Gladstone, 105; to await issue, 107; misapprehends situation, 114.
Tennyson, Alfred, Lord, 71; on Bright, 78.
Texas, annexation, 42.
Thomas, George Henry, 138.
Timeliness, important, 80.
Times, London, 19; supports the South, 69; influence of, 73; language of, 74; *Uncle Tom's Cabin*, 82.
Toombs, Robert, on 'Uncle Tom', 80.
Treaties, standing of, 51.
Treaty of Washington, 121.

Ulster, 177.
Uncle Tom's Cabin, influence of, 79, 82, 124, 159.
Union, dissolution of the, 42, 62.
United States, War of Secession, Bryce on, 10; important results, 13; Mill on, 19; memory of, 59.

Vicksburg, fall of, 145.
Victoria, Queen, 98.
Virginia and State's rights, 137; resolutions, 139.
Virginia, 16.

Washington, George, 36.
Washington, Treaty of, 121.
Wilderness, campaign in, 153.
William of Orange, 141.
Wilmington, N. C., 161.
Wilson, Woodrow, President, 27.
Wolseley, Garnet, Lord, 119, 175.

Oxford : Printed at the Clarendon Press by Horace Hart